Developer
Web Links

COMPANION FOR DEVELOPERS

Idris Yusuf

DISCLAIMER

All links in this directory have been selected using the standard links protocol. Links are provided for information and convenience only. We cannot accept responsibility for the sites entered in this directory, or the information found there. A link does not imply an endorsement of a site; likewise, not having a particular link entered does not imply lack of endorsement. Further, by providing link to these sites is not an endorsement of any particular product, practice, service provider or institution, nor does it necessarily endorse views expressed or facts presented on these sites. In addition, Developer Web Links does not make any warranty, expressed or implied, or assumes any legal liability or responsibility for the accuracy, completeness, timing, or usefulness of any information linked to or from these sites.

The practices and information on those sites are beyond our control. When linking to these sites, users are subject to the privacy practices of that new site. Developer Web Links Team is not responsible for them.

Addition and Removal of links

Developer Web Links reserves the right, at its sole discretion, to add or remove any web link.

TRADEMARKS

All entries in this directory are trademarks or registered trademarks of their respective companies in the United States and/or other countries.

ABOUT THE AUTHOR

Idris Yusuf began his education in computing at the Yaba College of Technology as a Computer Science student and there he earned National Diploma. He moved on to University of Lagos ,where he earned B.Sc(Hons) in Computer Science. He also won the most Innovative Prize Award as a member of a team at the Microsoft Imagine Cup Nigeria Finals, twice.

DEDICATION

To all developers

TABLE OF CONTENTS

ACCESSORIES

Adesso	http://www.adesso.com
Antec	http://www.antec.com
Aquapac	http://www.aquapac.net
BBP Bags	http://www.bbpbags.com
Built NY	http://www.builtny.com
Case Logic	http://www.caselogic.com
CaseCrown	http://www.casecrown.com
CineBags	http://www.cinebags.com
Creative	http://www.creative.com
Crumpler	http://www.crumpler.com
Deepcool	http://www.deepcool-us.com
Gear Head	http://www.pcgearhead.com
Golla	http://www.golla.com
Gyration	http://www.gyration.com
Hauppauge	http://www.hauppauge.com
IMicro	http://www.imicro.com
Incase	http://www.goincase.com

Kata	http://www.kata-bags.com
Kensington	http://us.kensington.com/
Logitech	http://www.logitech.com
Masscool	http://www.masscool.com
OtterBox	http://www.otterbox.com
Razer	http://www.razerzone.com
Samsonite	http://www.samsonite.com
Slappa	http://www.slappa.com
Speck	http://www.speckproducts.com
Tamrac	http://www.tamrac.com
Targus	http://www.targus.com
TeleAdapt	http://www.teleadapt.com
Timbuk2	http://www.timbuk2.com

ANIMATION

Adobe After Effects	http://www.adobe.com/products/aftereffects.html
Adobe Flash Professional	http://www.adobe.com/products/flash.html
Anime Studio	http://anime.smithmicro.com/

Away3D	http://www.away3d.com
Evermotion	http://www.evermotion.org
Honest Technology	http://www.honestech.com/main/index.asp
KoolMoves	http://www.koolmoves.com
MAXON	http://www.maxon.net
Pixar	http://www.pixar.com
Poser Pro	http://poser.smithmicro.com/poserpro.html
Reallusion	http://www.reallusion.com
Silverlight	http://www.silverlight.net
Toon Boom	http://www.toonboom.com
Ulead	http://www.ulead.com
Xara	http://www.xara.com

ANTIVIRUS/INTERNET SECURITY

Ad-Aware	http://www.lavasoft.com
Agnitum	http://www.agnitum.com
ArcVir	http://www.arcabit.com
Availasoft	http://www.availasoft.com

Avast	http://www.avast.com
AVG	http://www.avg.com
Avira	http://www.avira.com
BitDefender	http://www.bitdefender.com
BullGuard	http://www.bullguard.com
Comodo	http://www.comodo.com
Coranti	http://www.coranti.com
Digital-Defender	http://www.digital-defender.com
Emsisoft	http://www.emsisoft.com/en/
eScan	http://www.escanav.com/english/
ESET	http://www.eset.com
Faronics	http://www.faronics.com
Faronics	http://www.faronics.com
F-PROT	http://www.f-prot.com
F-Secure	http://www.f-secure.com
G Data	http://www.gdata-software.com
K7	http://www.k7computing.com
Kaspersky	http://www.kaspersky.com

Lavasoft	http://www.lavasoft.com
Lumension	http://www.lumension.com
Malwarebytes	http://www.malwarebytes.org
Microsoft Forefront	http://www.microsoft.com/forefront/
Microsoft Security Essentials	http://www.microsoft.com/en-us/security_essentials/default.aspx
Norman	http://www.norman.com
OPSWAT	http://www.opswat.com
Panda Security	http://www.pandasecurity.com
PC Tools	http://www.pctools.com
Quick Heal	http://www.quickheal.com
Rising	http://www.rising-global.com
Sophos	http://www.sophos.com/en-us/
SPAMfighter	http://www.spamfighter.com
Symantec	http://www.symantec.com
Trend Micro	http://www.trendmicro.com
TrustPort	http://www.trustport.com/en
UnThreat	http://www.unthreat.com
VirusBuster	http://www.virusbuster.hu/en

Webroot	http://www.webroot.com
WOT	http://www.mywot.com
ZoneAlarm	http://www.zonealarm.com

AUDIO

Akai	http://www.akai.com
AKG	http://www.akg.com
Altec Lansing	http://www.alteclansing.com
Audio-Technica	http://www.audio-technica.com
Auzentech	http://www.auzentech.com
Avid	http://www.avid.com
BEHRINGER	http://www.behringer.com
Beyerdynamic	http://www.beyerdynamic.com
Blue Microphones	http://www.bluemic.com
Bose	http://www.bose.com
Cables To Go	http://www.cablestogo.com
Creative	http://www.creative.com
CSR	http://www.csr.com

Denon	http://www.denon.com
Diamond Multimedia	http://www.diamondmm.com
Digigram	http://www.digigram.com
DYNEX	http://www.dynexproducts.com
Electro-Voice	http://www.electrovoice.com
Griffin Technology	http://www.griffintechnology.com
Intel HD Audio	http://www.intel.com/design/chipsets/hdaudio.htm
Jabra	http://www.jabra.com
JLab	http://www.jlabaudio.com
Klipsch	http://www.klipsch.com
Korg	http://www.korg.com
Koss	http://www.koss.com
M-Audio	http://www.m-audio.com
MXL	http://www.mxlmics.com
Nady	http://www.nady.com
Nuforce	http://www.nuforce.com
Phillips	http://www.philips.com
Pinnacle Systems	http://www.pinnaclesys.com

Plantronics	http://www.plantronics.com
Polk Audio	http://www.polkaudio.com
Rocketfish	http://www.rocketfishproducts.com
Sabrent	http://www.sabrent.com
Sennheiser	http://www.sennheiser.com
Shure	http://www.shure.com
SIIG	http://www.siig.com
Tascam	http://www.tascam.com
VXi Corporation	http://www.vxicorp.com

BIOMETRICS

AuthenTec	http://www.authentec.com/
BioLink	http://www.biolinksolutions.com
Cross Match	http://www.crossmatch.com
Dakty	http://www.dakty.com
DERMALOG	http://www.dermalog.de
DigitalPersona	http://www.digitalpersona.com
L-1	http://www.l1id.com

Lumidigm	http://www.lumidigm.com
Neurotechnology	http://www.neurotechnology.com
SecuGen	http://www.secugen.com

BOOKS

Adobe Books	http://www.adobe.com/training/books/
AMACOM Books	http://www.amacombooks.org
Apress	http://www.apress.com
Artech House	http://www.artechhouse.com
Berrett-Koehler	http://www.bkconnection.com
Books24x7	http://www.books24x7.com
BrainySoftware	http://books.brainysoftware.com/
Cambridge University Press	http://www.cambridge.org
Career Press	http://www.careerpress.com
Cengage	http://www.cengage.com
Cisco Press	http://www.ciscopress.com
Class on Demand	http://www.classondemand.net
Course Technology	http://www.courseptr.com

PTR	
CRC Press	http://www.crcpress.com
CreateSpace	https://www.createspace.com
Deitel	http://www.deitel.com
Dummies	http://www.dummies.com
Elsevier	http://www.elsevier.com
Focal Press	http://www.focalpress.com
FT Press	http://www.ftpress.com
Havard University Press	http://www.hup.harvard.edu/
Head First	http://www.headfirstlabs.com
Hindawi	http://www.hindawi.com
IBM Press	http://www.ibm.com/ibmpress
InformIT	http://www.informit.com
Jones & Bartlett Learning	http://www.jblearning.com
Lammle Press	http://www.lammlepress.com
LexisNexis	http://www.lexisnexis.com
Macmillan	http://www.macmillan.com

Manning	http://www.manning.com
McGraw-Hill	http://www.mcgraw-hill.com
Microsoft Press	http://www.microsoft.com/mspress/
MIT Press	http://mitpress.mit.edu/
Murach	http://www.murach.com
No Starch Press	http://www.nostarch.com
O'Reilly	http://www.oreilly.com
Oxford University Press	http://www.oup.com
Packt Publishing	http://www.packtpub.com
Peachpit Press	http://www.peachpit.com
Pragmatic Programmers	http://www.pragprog.com
QUE	http://www.quepublishing.com
Rocky Nook	http://www.rockynook.com
Routledge	http://www.routledge.com
Safari Books Online	http://www.safaribooksonline.com
SAP Press	http://www.sap-press.com
SAS Publishing	http://support.sas.com/publishing/index.html

Springer	http://www.springer.com
Stanford University Press	http://www.sup.org
SYBEX	http://www.sybex.com
Syngress	http://www.syngress.com
Talented Pixie	http://www.talentedpixie.com
Taylor & Francis	http://www.taylorandfrancis.com
Wiley	http://www.wiley.com
Wrox Press	http://www.wrox.com

BUSINESS

Accenture	http://www.accenture.com
Acumatica	http://www.acumatica.com
Amdocs	http://www.amdocs.com
Autonomy	http://www.autonomy.com
Autotask	http://www.autotask.com
Avanade	http://www.avanade.com
CA Technologies	http://www.ca.com
Canonical	http://www.canonical.com

Capgemini	http://www.capgemini.com
ClickSoftware	http://www.clicksoftware.com
Cognizant	http://www.cognizant.com
Compuware	http://www.compuware.com
CSC	http://www.csc.com
Deloitte	http://www.deloitte.com
Domo	http://www.domo.com
Enloop	http://www.enloop.com
Epicor	http://www.epicor.com
Equinix	http://www.equinix.com
Ernst & Young	http://www.ey.com
F5	http://www.f5.com
ftopia	http://www.ftopia.com
Hitachi Consulting	http://www.hitachiconsulting.com
iGATE Patni	http://www.igatepatni.com
Imperva	http://www.imperva.com
Infosys	http://www.infosys.com
Jaspersoft	http://www.jaspersoft.com

KnowledgeTree	http://www.knowledgetree.com
KPMG	http://www.kpmg.com
Level Platforms	http://www.levelplatforms.com
Liferay	http://www.liferay.com
McKinsey	http://www.mckinsey.com
MicroStrategy	http://www.microstrategy.com
Ness	http://www.ness.com
NetStandard	http://www.netstandard.com
Novell	http://www.novell.com
Oracle	http://www.oracle.com
Pentaho	http://www.pentaho.com
PwC	http://www.pwc.com
Rocket Software	http://www.rocketsoftware.com
SAP	http://www.sap.com
SAS	http://www.sas.com
ScaleOut	http://www.scaleoutsoftware.com
Smith Micro	http://www.smithmicro.com
SugarCRM	http://www.sugarcrm.com

SumTotal	http://www.sumtotalsystems.com
SupportSpace	http://corporate.supportspace.com/
Sybase	http://www.sybase.com
Taleo	http://www.taleo.com
TATA Consultancy Services	http://www.tcs.com
TIBCO	http://www.tibco.com
Unisys	http://www.unisys.com
Wipro	http://www.wipro.com
Worksoft	http://www.worksoft.com

CERTIFICATION

Adobe Certified	http://www.adobe.com/support/certification/
APM Group	http://www.apmg-international.com
Boson	http://www.boson.com
CertificationBooks.com	http://www.certificationbooks.com
Certified Internet Webmaster	http://www.ciwcertified.com
Certified Wireless Network Professional (CWNP)	http://www.cwnp.com
Certiport	http://www.certiport.com

CompTIA	http://www.comptia.org
DevelopMentor	http://www.develop.com
EC Council	http://www.eccouncil.org
ECDL Foundation	http://www.ecdl.com
EDULEARN	http://www.edulearn.com
GIAC - Global Information Assurance Certification	http://www.giac.org
Global Information Assurance Certification (GIAC)	http://www.giac.org
GoCertify	http://www.gocertify.com
GoExam	http://www.goexam.com
Graduate Management Admissions Test - GMAT	http://www.mba.com/mba/Takethe GMAT
Guidance Software	http://www.guidancesoftware.com
Human Resource Certification Institute	http://www.hrci.org
IEEE Biometrics Certification	http://www.ieeebiometricscertificati on.org
Information Systems Audit and Control Association	http://www.isaca.org
Information Technology Certification Council (ITCC)	http://www.itcertcouncil.org

ITIL	http://www.itil-officialsite.com
LearnCertNow.com	http://www.learncertnow.com
Learning Tree	http://www.learningtree.com
Linux Professional Institute (LPI)	http://www.lpi.org
MeasureUp	http://www.measureup.com
Microsoft Certification	http://microsoft.com/learning/en/us/certification/cert-overview.aspx
Novell Certifications	http://www.novell.com/training/certinfo/
Oracle University	http://education.oracle.com/
Pass4sure	http://www.pass4sure.com
Pearson VUE	http://www.vue.com
PRINCE2	http://www.prince2.com
Project Management Institute	http://www.pmi.org
Prometric	http://www.prometric.com
RHCE	http://www.redhat.com/certification/rhce/
RouterSim	http://www.routersim.com
SAS 70	http://www.sas70.com
TrainSignal	http://www.trainsignal.com
Transcender	http://www.transcender.com

uCertify	http://www.ucertify.com
VeriTest Certification Programs	http://en-us.lionbridge.com/product-engineering/product-certification/default.htm
VMTraining	http://www.vmtraining.net

CLOUD COMPUTING

3Tera	http://www.3tera.com
Amazon Cloud Drive	https://www.amazon.com/clouddrive/learnmore
Apica	http://www.apicasystem.com
Apigee	http://www.apigee.com
AppDynamics	http://www.appdynamics.com
Appirio	http://www.appirio.com
Apple iCloud	http://www.apple.com/icloud/
Apprenda	http://www.apprenda.com
Asigra	http://www.asigra.com
BlueLock	http://www.bluelock.com
BMC	http://www.bmc.com
Caringo	http://www.caringo.com
Cirrascale	http://www.cirrascale.com

Citrix	http://www.citrix.com
Cloud Aspects	http://www.cloudaspects.com
Cloud Cruiser	http://www.cloudcruiser.com
Cloud Foundry	http://www.cloudfoundry.com
Cloud9 Real Time	http://www.cloud9realtime.com
Cloudability	http://www.cloudability.com
CloudBees	http://www.cloudbees.com
CloudSigma	http://www.cloudsigma.com
CollabNet	http://www.collab.net
CopperEgg	http://www.copperegg.com
DotCloud	http://www.dotcloud.com
ElasticHosts	http://www.elastichosts.com
Electric Cloud	http://www.electric-cloud.com
EMC	http://www.emc.com
Engine Yard	http://www.engineyard.com
ENKI	http://www.enki.co
enStratus	http://www.enstratus.com
Eucalyptus Systems	http://www.eucalyptus.com

Funambol	http://www.funambol.com
GoGrid	http://www.gogrid.com
GridGain	http://www.gridgain.com
GuardTime	http://www.guardtime.com
Heroku	http://www.heroku.com
Hexagrid	http://www.hexagrid.com
Hosting.com	http://www.hosting.com
Intalio	http://www.intalio.com
Intel Cloud Builders	http://www.intelcloudbuilders.com
IP Commerce	http://www.ipcommerce.com
Joyent	http://www.joyent.com
m2mi	http://www.m2mi.com
Mezeo	http://www.mezeo.com
Microsoft SkyDrive	http://explore.live.com/windows-live-skydrive
MuleSoft	http://www.mulesoft.com
Nasuni	http://www.nasuni.com
newScale	http://www.newscale.com
Nimbula	http://www.nimbula.com

Nirvanix	http://www.nirvanix.com
OpenStack	http://www.openstack.org
Opscode	http://www.opscode.com
OpSource	http://www.opsource.net
Panda Security	http://www.pandasecurity.com
Ping Identity	https://www.pingidentity.com
Platform Computing	http://www.platform.com
Primadesk	https://www.primadesk.com
Rackspace	http://www.rackspace.com
RightScale	http://www.rightscale.com
rPath	http://www.rpath.com
Salesforce	http://www.salesforce.com
ScaleXtreme	http://www.scalextreme.com
Scality	http://www.scality.com
SGI	http://www.sgi.com
Skytap	http://www.skytap.com
SMEStorage	http://www.smestorage.com
SOASTA	http://www.soasta.com

SoftLayer	http://www.softlayer.com
Software AG	http://www.softwareag.com
SQL Azure	http://www.microsoft.com/windowsazure/sql azure/
Symantec.cloud	http://www.symanteccloud.com
Terremark	http://www.terremark.com
Twilio	http://www.twilio.com
Windows Azure	http://www.microsoft.com/windowsazure/
Wyse	http://www.wyse.com
Zenoss	http://www.zenoss.com

COMMUNICATION

4PSA	http://www.4psa.com
Aastra	http://www.aastra.com
Adax	http://www.adax.com
Alcatel-Lucent	http://www.alcatel-lucent.com
Ascom	http://www.ascom.com
Asterisk	http://www.asterisk.org
AT&T	http://www.att.com

Avaya	http://www.avaya.com
AVI-SPL	http://www.avispl.com
Avistar	http://www.avistar.com
Biscom	http://www.biscom.com
Boingo	http://www.boingo.com
Broadcom	http://www.broadcom.com
Broadvox	http://www.broadvox.com
CenturyLink	http://www.centurylink.com
Chelsio	http://www.chelsio.com
Cisco	http://www.cisco.com
Cisco WebEx	http://www.webex.com
ClearOne	http://www.clearone.com
CommuniGate	http://www.communigate.com
ConferTel	http://www.confertel.net
CounterPath	http://www.counterpath.com
CyberData	http://www.cyberdata.net
Dialogic	http://www.dialogic.com
Digium	http://www.digium.com/en/

EasyChair	https://www.easychair.org
Ericsson	http://www.ericsson.com
Ezenia!	http://www.ezenia.com
FreePBX	http://www.freepbx.org
FreeSWITCH	http://www.freeswitch.org
GoToMeeting	http://www.gotomeeting.com
Grandstream	http://www.grandstream.com
Huawei	http://www.huawei.com/en/
IBM Lotus Software	http://www.ibm.com/software/lotus/
Ifbyphone	http://public.ifbyphone.com/
Interactive Intelligence	http://www.inin.com
LG-Ericsson	http://www.lgericsson.com
LiveChat	http://www.livechatinc.com
LivePerson	http://www.liveperson.com
MegaMeeting	http://www.megameeting.com
Microsoft Lync	http://www.microsoft.com/communicationsserver/
Mitel	http://www.mitel.com
Motorola	http://www.motorola.com

NEC	http://www.nec.com
Nefsis	http://www.nefsis.com
Network Equipment Technologies	http://www.net.com
Nokia Siemens Networks	http://www.nokiasiemensnetworks.com
Nortel	http://www.nortel.com
NTT DOCOMO	http://www.nttdocomo.com
O2	http://www.o2.co.uk
OnSIP	http://www.onsip.com
OpenSIPS	http://www.opensips.org
Orange	http://www.orange.com/en_EN/
Qualcomm	http://www.qualcomm.com
RADVISION	http://www.radvision.com
Revolabs	http://www.revolabs.com
Rogers	http://www.rogers.com
ShoreTel	http://www.shoretel.com
Siemens	http://www.siemens.com
Sipera	http://www.sipera.com

SIPfoundry	http://www.sipfoundry.org
snom	http://www.snom.com
Sprint	http://www.sprint.com
TalkPoint	http://www.talkpointcommunications.com
Tango	http://www.tango.me
Tixeo	http://www.tixeo.com
TracFone	http://www.tracfone.com
TrueConf	http://www.trueconf.com
U.S. Cellular	http://www.uscellular.com
Verizon	http://www.verizon.com
VideoMost	http://www.videomost.com
Vidtel	http://www.vidtel.com
Virgin Mobile	http://www.virginmobile.com
Vocera	http://www.vocera.com
Vodafone	http://www.vodafone.com
Zetron	http://www.zetron.com
Zultys	http://www.zultys.com

COMMUNITY

ASP.NET Community	http://www.asp.net/community
Autodesk User Group International – AUGI	http://www.augi.com
bada Developer	http://developer.bada.com/
Bitbucket	https://bitbucket.org/
BlackBerry Developer Zone	http://us.blackberry.com/developers/
Codecademy	http://www.codecademy.com
CodeEval	http://www.codeeval.com
CodeGallery	http://code.msdn.microsoft.com/
CodeGuru	http://www.codeguru.com
Codehaus	http://www.codehaus.org
CodePlex	http://www.codeplex.com
Developer.com	http://www.developer.com
DevX	http://www.devx.com
eBay Developers Program	http://developer.ebay.com/
Elance	http://www.elance.com
Facebook Developers	http://developers.facebook.com/
Forrst	http://www.forrst.com

Java Community Process – JCP	http://www.jcp.org/en/home/index
Launchpad	https://www.launchpad.net
Linux Developer Network	http://ldn.linuxfoundation.org/
MIX	http://www.visitmix.com/
Motorola Developer Network	http://developer.motorola.com/
MSDN – Microsoft Developer Network	http://msdn.microsoft.com/en-us/default.aspx
Nokia Developer	http://www.developer.nokia.com/
Oracle Application User Group	http://www.oaug.org
Perl Foundation	http://www.perlfoundation.org
Quest International Users Group	http://www.questdirect.org
Robots Podcast	http://www.robotspodcast.com
RubyGems.org	http://www.rubygems.org
Samsung Mobile Developer	http://developers.samsungmobile.com/
SenchaDevs	http://www.senchadevs.com
Sony Ericsson Developer World	http://developer.sonyericsson.com/
Sourceforge.net	http://www.sourceforge.net
Sprint Application Developer	http://developer.sprint.com/
StackOverflow	http://www.stackoverflow.com

Twitter Developers	https://dev.twitter.com/
Visual Studio Gallery	http://www.visualstudiogallery.com
Wrox Programmer Forums	http://p2p.wrox.com/

COMPUTER

Acer	http://www.acer.com
Alienware	http://www.alienware.com
Apple	http://www.apple.com
Asus	http://www.asus.com
Chromebook	http://www.google.com/chromebook/
Cisco Cius	http://cisco.com/en/US/products/ps11156/index.html
Compaq	http://www.compaq.com
Dell	http://www.dell.com
Digital Storm	http://www.digitalstormonline.com
eMachines	http://www.emachines.com
Eurocom	http://www.eurocom.com
Fujitsu	http://www.fujitsu.com
Gateway	http://www.gateway.com

General Dynamics Itronix	http://www.gd-itronix.com
GIGABYTE	http://www.gigabyte.com
Hi-Grade	http://www.higrade.com
HP	http://www.hp.com
iBUYPOWER	http://www.ibuypower.com
IGEL	http://www.igel.com
Lenovo	http://www.lenovo.com
Maingear	http://www.maingear.com
MSI	http://www.msi.com
Packard Bell	http://www.packardbell.com
Panasonic	http://www.panasonic.com
Rain Computers	http://www.raincomputers.com
Samsung	http://www.samsung.com
Shuttle	http://www.shuttle.com
Sony	http://www.sony.com
Toshiba	http://www.toshiba.com
Velocity Micro	http://www.velocitymicro.com

CONTENT MANAGEMENT

Alfresco	http://www.alfresco.com
Box.net	http://www.box.net
CMS Made Simple	http://www.cmsmadesimple.org
cmsbox	http://www.cmsbox.com/en/cms
Concrete5	http://www.concrete5.org
DotNetNuke	http://www.dotnetnuke.com
Drupal	http://www.drupal.org
Ektron	http://www.ektron.com
Joomla	http://www.joomla.org
Kentico	http://www.kentico.com
Liferay	http://www.liferay.com
Midgard CMS	http://www.midgard-project.org
MODx	http://www.modx.com
Mongolia CMS	http://www.magnolia-cms.com
OpenCms	http://www.opencms.org/en/
OpenText	http://www.opentext.com
Plone	http://www.plone.org

Radiant CMS	http://www.radiantcms.org
Saperion	http://www.saperion.com/en/
SilverStripe	http://www.silverstripe.com
Simple Machines Forum	http://www.simplemachines.org
Structr	http://www.structr.org
TYPO3	http://www.typo3.org
Umbraco	http://www.umbraco.com
WebGUI	http://www.webgui.org
XOOPS	http://www.xoops.org

DATA

A10 Networks	http://www.a10networks.com
Acronis	http://www.acronis.com
Altaro	http://www.altaro.com
AppAssure	http://www.appassure.com
Aster Data	http://www.asterdata.com
Atempo	http://www.atempo.com
BakBone	http://www.bakbone.com

Bull	http://www.bull.com
Cloudera	http://www.cloudera.com
Dasher Technologies	http://www.dasher.com
Datameer	http://www.datameer.com
DataStax	http://www.datastax.com
Datto	http://www.dattobackup.com
Digital Reasoning	http://www.digitalreasoning.com
Dimension Data	http://www.dimensiondata.com
Druva	http://www.druva.com
Egenera	http://www.egenera.com
Exagrid	http://www.exagrid.com
Fortrust Datacenter	http://www.fortrustdatacenter.com
Fusion-io	http://www.fusionio.com
GigaSpaces	http://www.gigaspaces.com
GNAX	http://www.gnax.com
Greenplum	http://www.greenplum.com
Hitachi Data Systems	http://www.hds.com
i365	http://www.i365.com

Infobright	http://www.infobright.com
Informatica	http://www.informatica.com
Information Builders	http://www.informationbuilders.com
Ingres	http://www.ingres.com
Interxion	http://www.interxion.com
Karmarsphere	http://www.karmasphere.com
Momentum SI	http://www.momentumsi.com
Mozy	http://www.mozy.com
Neotix	http://www.noetix.com
NetApp	http://www.netapp.com
Netezza	http://www.netezza.com
OSIsoft	http://www.osisoft.com
Permabit	http://www.permabit.com
PKWARE	http://www.pkware.com
Qlogic	http://www.qlogic.com
R1Soft	http://www.r1soft.com
Raritan	http://www.raritan.com
Simba Technologies	http://www.simba.com

Splunk	http://www.splunk.com
StoredIQ	http://www.storediq.com
Syncsort	http://www.syncsort.com
Tableau Software	http://www.tableausoftware.com
Talend	http://www.talend.com
Teradata	http://www.teradata.com
Tervela	http://www.tervela.com
TwinStrata	http://www.twinstrata.com
Unitrends	http://www.unitrends.com
Versant	http://www.versant.com
Vertica	http://www.vertica.com
Vision Solutions	http://www.visionsolutions.com
Zmanda	http://www.zmanda.com

DATABASE

Acxiom	http://www.acxiom.com
Allround Automations	http://www.allroundautomations.com
Amazon SimpleDB	http://aws.amazon.com/simpledb/

Apache CouchDB	http://couchdb.apache.org/
ApexSQL	http://www.apexsql.com
Couchbase	http://www.couchbase.com
CUBRID	http://www.cubrid.org
Embarcadero	http://www.embarcadero.com
EnterpriseDB	http://www.enterprisedb.com
FileMaker	http://www.filemaker.com
HBase	http://hbase.apache.org/
HSQLDB	http://www.hsqldb.org
IBM DB2	http://www.ibm.com/software/data/db2/
IBM Informix	http://www.ibm.com/software/data/informix/
InterSystems Caché	http://www.intersystems.com/cache/
Intuit Quickbase	http://quickbase.intuit.com/
Microsoft SQL Server	http://www.microsoft.com/sqlserver/
MongoDB	http://www.mongodb.org
MySQL	http://www.mysql.com
Neo4j	http://www.neo4j.org
OpenTSDB	http://www.opentsdb.net

Oracle Berkeley DB	http://oracle.com/us/products/database/berkeley-db/index.html
Pervasive Software	http://www.pervasive.com
PostgreSQL	http://www.postgresql.org
QuantumDB	http://quantum.sourceforge.net/
Quest Software	http://www.quest.com
Raven DB	http://www.ravendb.net
Redis	http://www.redis.io
ScaleBase	http://www.scalebase.com
SQL Buddy	http://www.sqlbuddy.com
SQLAlchemy	http://www.sqlalchemy.org
SQLite	http://www.sqlite.org
SQLstream	http://www.sqlstream.com
SQLyog	http://www.webyog.com
TrackVia	http://www.trackvia.com
VoltDB	http://www.voltdb.com

DEVELOPMENT TOOLS

37signals	http://www.37signals.com

Aconex	http://www.aconex.com
Adobe Flex	http://www.flex.org
Amanuens	http://www.amanuens.com
ANTLR	http://www.antlr.org
Apache	http://www.apache.org
Apache ActiveMQ	http://activemq.apache.org/
Apache Maven	http://maven.apache.org/
AppDev	http://www.appdev.com
Arquillian	http://www.jboss.org/arquillian
Aspose	http://www.aspose.com
Atlassian	http://www.atlassian.com
Basecamp	http://www.basecamphq.com
Bazaar	http://bazaar.canonical.com/en/
Beanstalk	http://www.beanstalkapp.com
bitly	http://bit.ly/
Borland	http://www.borland.com
Bugzilla	http://www.bugzilla.org
Cacti	http://www.cacti.net

Central Desktop	http://www.centraldesktop.com
Cloudera	http://www.cloudera.com
Codefold	http://plugins.netbeans.org/plugin/35534/codefold
Crate	http://www.letscrate.com
Cropper	http://cropper.codeplex.com/
cURL	http://curl.haxx.se/
dbTools	http://www.dbtools.com.br/EN/
Devart	http://www.devart.com
DevExpress	http://www.devexpress.com
Dropbox	https://www.dropbox.com
Dxperience	http://devexpress.com/Subscriptions/DXperience/
Electric Cloud	http://www.electric-cloud.com
Embarcadero	http://www.embarcadero.com
Evident Software	http://www.evidentsoftware.com
FileZilla	http://www.filezilla-project.org
FlashFXP	http://www.flashfxp.com
Fog Creek	http://www.fogcreek.com
Font Bureau	http://www.fontbureau.com

FontShop	http://www.fontshop.com
Fortify	https://www.fortify.com
FXRuby	http://www.fxruby.org
GCC – GNU Compiler Collection	http://gcc.gnu.org/
GlobalSCAPE	http://www.globalscape.com
Google App Engine	http://code.google.com/appengine/
Google Earth KML	http://code.google.com/apis/kml/documentation/
Google URL Shortner	http://goo.gl/
Hadoop	http://hadoop.apache.org/
HeidiSQL	http://www.heidisql.com
Hot Scripts	http://www.hotscripts.com
IBM developerWorks	http://www.ibm.com/developerworks/
IBM Rational Software	http://www.ibm.com/software/rational/
Infragistics	http://www.infragistics.com
InishTech	http://www.inishtech.com
Ipswitch	http://www.ipswitch.com
Java SE	http://www.oracle.com/technetwork/java/javase/downloads/index.html
JavaFX	http://www.javafx.com

JBoss Drools	http://www.jboss.org/drools/
Jenkins	http://www.jenkins-ci.org
JetBrains	http://www.jetbrains.com
JetBrains MPS – Meta Programming System	http://www.jetbrains.com/mps/index.html
JetBrains ReSharper	http://www.jetbrains.com/resharper/index.html
JetBrains TeamCity	http://www.jetbrains.com/teamcity/
JIRA	http://www.atlassian.com/software/jira/
JUnit	http://junit.sourceforge.net/
K2	http://www.k2.com
KDE	http://www.kde.org
LaTeX	http://www.latex-project.org
Lightweight User Interface Toolkit (LWUIT)	http://lwuit.java.net/
Lionbridge	http://en-us.lionbridge.com/Default.aspx
Loquendo	http://www.loquendo.com/en/
Lymbix	http://www.lymbix.com
Microsoft .Net	http://www.microsoft.com/net/
Microsoft Dreamspark	http://www.dreamspark.com

Microsoft Expression	http://www.microsoft.com/expression/
Microsoft Patterns & Practices	http://msdn.microsoft.com/en-us/practices/default.aspx
Microsoft Project	http://www.microsoft.com/project/
Microsoft Silverlight	http://www.microsoft.com/silverlight/
MongoHQ	https://www.mongohq.com
MSBuild	http://msdn.microsoft.com/en-us/library/0k6kkbsd.aspx
MyDB Studio	http://www.mydb-studio.com
MySQL Workbench	http://wb.mysql.com/
Natural Language Toolkit	http://www.nltk.org
Navicat	http://www.navicat.com
Ncover	http://www.ncover.com
Ness	http://www.ness.com
NHibernate	http://nhforge.org/Default.aspx
NHibernate Profiler	http://www.nhprof.com
NuCaptcha	http://www.nucaptcha.com
NUnit	http://www.nunit.org
OAuth	http://www.oauth.net
OCS Inventory NG	http://www.ocsinventory-ng.org/en/

OneLogin	http://www.onelogin.com
OPSWAT	http://www.opswat.com
Pivotal Tracker	http://www.pivotaltracker.com
PreEmptive Solutions	http://www.preemptive.com
ProgrammableWeb. com	http://www.programmableweb.com
PTC	http://www.ptc.com
Puppet	http://www.puppetlabs.com
QualityLogic	http://www.qualitylogic.com
Quantitative Software Management	http://www.qsm.com
RabbitMQ	http://www.rabbitmq.com
Rovi	http://www.rovicorp.com
SAManage	http://www.samanage.com
Saplo	http://www.saplo.com
ScalaTest	http://www.scalatest.org
Search Technologies	http://www.searchtechnologies.com
Selenium	http://www.seleniumhq.org
Sequel Pro	http://www.sequelpro.com

Simba Technologies	http://www.simba.com
SIMULIA	http://www.simulia.com
SmartFTP	http://www.smartftp.com
Sogeti	http://www.sogeti.com
Soonr	http://www.soonr.com
SQL Maestro	http://www.sqlmaestro.com
SQLWave	http://www.nerocode.com
Tagstand	http://www.tagstand.com
TechSmith	http://www.techsmith.com
Telerik	http://www.telerik.com
TestNG	http://www.testng.org
TIBCO	http://www.tibco.com
Tigris	http://www.tigris.org
Tiny URL	http://www.tiny.cc
Toad	http://www.quest.com/toad/
TortoiseSVN	http://www.tortoisesvn.net
Twitter Bootstrap	http://twitter.github.com/bootstrap/
Typekit	http://www.typekit.com

uTest	http://www.utest.com
VisualSVN	http://www.visualsvn.com
VueScan	http://www.hamrick.com
WampServer	http://www.wampserver.com
wave-vs.net	http://www.wave-vs.net
Webdrive	http://www.webdrive.com
Webtype	http://www.webtype.com
Webyog	http://www.webyog.com/en/
Windows Presentation Foundation (WPF)	http://windowsclient.net/WPF/
WinSCP	http://winscp.net/eng/index.php
WSO2	http://www.wso2.com
Yahoo! Media Player	http://mediaplayer.yahoo.com/
Zephyr	http://www.getzephyr.com

E-COMMERCE

ActiveCampaign	http://www.activecampaign.com
Ad Age	http://www.adage.com
Ad Council	http://www.adcouncil.org

adBrite	http://www.adbrite.com
AdChoice	http://www.adchoiceinc.com
AdMarvel	http://www.admarvel.com
Ads of the World	http://www.adsoftheworld.com
AisleBuyer	http://www.aislebuyer.com
Amazon Payments	https://payments.amazon.com/
American Express	https://home.americanexpress.com
Apache ofBiz	http://ofbiz.apache.org/
AppNexus	http://www.appnexus.com
Assistly	http://www.assistly.com
AuditMyBooks	http://www.auditmybooks.com
Authorize.net	http://www.authorize.net
Backbase	http://www.backbase.com
BatchBlue	http://www.batchblue.com
BidVertiser	http://www.bidvertiser.com
BigCommerce	http://www.bigcommerce.com
Bill Me Later	https://www.billmelater.com
Bill.com	http://www.bill.com

BillGuard	http://www.billguard.com
BrightRoll	http://www.brightroll.com
Campaign Monitor	http://www.campaignmonitor.com
cashU	https://www.cashu.com
ChannelAdvisor	http://www.channeladvisor.com
Chitika	http://www.chitika.com
Comodo	http://www.comodo.com
Constant Contact	http://www.constantcontact.com
Demandbase	http://www.demandbase.com
DHL	http://www.dhl.com
Digital River	http://www.digitalriver.com
Discover Card	http://www.discovercard.com
Doba	http://www.doba.com
DoubleClick	http://www.doubleclick.com
Eloqua	http://www.eloqua.com
Empirical Path	http://www.empiricalpath.com
Entrust	http://www.entrust.net
E-Similate	http://www.e-similate.com

ExactTarget	http://www.exacttarget.com
Facebook Ads	http://www.facebook.com/advertising/
FedEx	http://www.fedex.com
First Data	http://www.firstdata.com
FreshBooks	http://www.freshbooks.com
Gemalto	http://www.gemalto.com
GeoTrust	http://www.geotrust.com
Get Satisfaction	http://www.getsatisfaction.com
GNUCash	http://www.gnucash.org
GoodData	http://www.gooddata.com
Google AdSense	https://www.google.com/adsense/
Google AdWords	http://adwords.google.com/
Google Wallet	http://www.google.com/wallet/
Hypercom	http://www.hypercom.com
InMobi	http://www.inmobi.com
InsideView	http://www.insideview.com
Intacct	http://www.intacct.com
Intuit	http://www.intuit.com

JobThread	http://www.jobthread.com
Liberty Reserve	http://www.libertyreserve.com
Magento	http://www.magentocommerce.com
Marketsync	http://www.marketsync.com
MasterCard	http://www.mastercard.com
McAfee Secure	http://www.mcafeesecure.com
MediaMath	http://www.mediamath.com
Microsoft Advertising	http://advertising.microsoft.com/
Mobclix	http://www.mobclix.com
Mobile Marketing Association	http://www.mmaglobal.com
mobileStorm	http://www.mobilestorm.com
Mojiva	http://www.mojiva.com
Moneybookers	http://www.moneybookers.com
MoPub	http://www.mopub.com
NetSuite	http://www.netsuite.com
Nexage	http://www.nexage.com
OpenCart	http://www.opencart.com
OpenSSL	http://www.openssl.org

OpinionLab	http://www.opinionlab.com
osCommerce	http://www.oscommerce.com
PayPal	http://www.paypal.com
PCI Security Standards Council	https://www.pcisecuritystandards.org
Pentaho	http://www.pentaho.com
Placecast	http://www.placecast.net
Pointroll	http://www.pointroll.com
PrestaShop	http://www.prestashop.com
Profitably	http://www.profitably.com
Qualys	http://www.qualys.com
QuickBooks	http://quickbooks.intuit.com/
RapidSSL	http://www.rapidssl.com
Sage Pay	http://www.sagepay.com
Sage Peachtree	http://www.peachtree.com
Sage Simply Accounting	http://www.simplyaccounting.com
SecurityMetrics	https://www.securitymetrics.com
Selligent	http://www.selligent.com
Sendloop	http://www.sendloop.com

Shoeboxed	http://www.shoeboxed.com
Smaato	http://www.smaato.com
StrongMail	http://www.strongmail.com
SunGard	http://www.sungard.com
Tactile CRM	http://www.tactilecrm.com
TechValidate	http://www.techvalidate.com
TellApart	http://www.tellapart.com
Text Link Ads	http://www.text-link-ads.com
Trust Guard	http://www.trust-guard.com
TRUSTe	http://www.truste.com
Trustwave	https://www.trustwave.com
UPS	http://www.ups.com
USA ePay	http://www.usaepay.com
USPS	http://www.usps.com
Verisign	http://www.verisign.com
Vindicia	http://www.vindicia.com
VirtueMart	http://www.virtuemart.net
Visa	http://www.visa.com

Webgility	http://www.webgility.com
WordWatch	http://www.wordwatch.com
WOT (Web of Trust)	http://www.mywot.com
Yahoo! Advertising	http://advertising.yahoo.com/
Zen Cart	http://www.zen-cart.com
Zendesk	http://www.zendesk.com
Zoovy	https://www.zoovy.com
Zuora	http://www.zuora.com

EDITOR/IDE

Anjuta DevStudio	http://projects.gnome.org/anjuta/
Aptana	http://www.aptana.com
BlackBerry Java Development Enviroment	http://us.blackberry.com/developers/javaappdev/javadevenv.jsp
Bluefish Editor	http://bluefish.openoffice.nl/
BlueJ	http://www.bluej.org
Cloud9 IDE	http://cloud9ide.com
CodeWarrior Development Studio	http://www.freescale.com/codewarrior

Eclipse	http://www.eclipse.org
Emacs	http://www.gnu.org/software/emacs/
Glade	http://glade.gnome.org/
IntelliJ IDEA	http://www.jetbrains.com/idea/
JCreator	http://www.jcreator.com
jEdit	http://www.jedit.org
JetBrains PyCharm	http://www.jetbrains.com/pycharm/index.html
JetBrains RubyMine	http://www.jetbrains.com/ruby/index.html
JetBrains WebStorm	http://www.jetbrains.com/webstorm/
jGRASP	http://www.jgrasp.org
Kdevelop	http://www.kdevelop.org
KompoZer	http://www.kompozer.net
Microsoft Visual Studio	http://www.microsoft.com/visualstudio/en-us
Miicrosoft Visual Studio	http://www.microsoft.com/visualstudio/en-us/home
MonoDevelop	http://www.mono-project.com
NetBeans	http://www.netbeans.org
Oracle Jdeveloper	http://www.oracle.com/technetwork/jdev/index.html
Qt Creator IDE	http://qt.nokia.com/products/developer-tools/

Real Studio	http://www.realsoftware.com/realstudio/
Selenium	http://www.seleniumhq.org
SharpDevelop	http://www.icsharpcode.net/OpenSource/SD/
SlickEdit	http://www.slickedit.com
Textpad	http://www.textpad.com
Ultimate++	http://www.ultimatepp.org
Vim	http://vim.sourceforge.net/
WaveMaker	http://www.wavemaker.com
Xcode	http://developer.apple.com/xcode/
Xemacs	http://www.xemacs.org
Xinha	http://www.xinha.org

E-HEALTH

Allscripts	http://www.allscripts.com
American Diabetes Association	http://www.diabetes.org
American Heart Association	http://www.americanheart.org
Axial Exchange	http://www.axialexchange.com
BodyMedia	http://www.bodymedia.com

BridgeHead Software	http://www.bridgeheadsoftware.com
Carestream	http://www.carestream.com
CIMIT	http://www.cimit.org
ClearCanvas	http://www.clearcanvas.ca
Continua Health Alliance	http://www.continuaalliance.org
EKHO	http://www.ekho.us
Fitbit	http://www.fitbit.com
FrontlineSMS	http://www.frontlinesms.com
InterSystems HealthShare	http://www.intersystems.com/healthshare/index.html
Johns Hopkins Medicine	http://www.hopkinsmedicine.org
McKesson	http://www.mckesson.com
Med Help	http://www.medhelp.org
MedApps	http://www.medapps.com
Medical Informatics Engineering	http://www.mieweb.com
Medtronic	http://www.medtronic.com
mHealth Alliance	http://www.mhealthalliance.org
Microlife	http://www.microlife.com

MotherKnows	http://www.motherknows.com
Nautilus	http://www.nautilus.com
Nonin	http://www.nonin.com
Nuesoft	http://www.nuesoft.com
OMRON	http://www.omron.com
OpenClinica	https://www.openclinica.com
OpenMRS	http://www.openmrs.org
Oregon Scientific	http://www.oregonscientific.com
Polar Electro	http://www.polar.fi/en/
Quantros	http://www.quantros.com
RunKeeper	http://www.runkeeper.com
Suunto	http://www.suunto.com
Tanita	http://www.tanita.com/en/
TriSano	http://www.trisano.com
UCLA Wireless Health	http://www.wirelesshealth.ucla.edu/
Voxiva	http://www.voxiva.com
West Wireless Health Institute	http://www.westwirelesshealth.org
Wireless Life-Sciences Alliance	http://www.wirelesslifesciences.org

World Health Organization (WHO)	http://www.who.int/en/

E-LEARNING

Absorb LMS	http://www.absorblms.com
Blackboard	http://www.blackboard.com
Chamilo	http://www.chamilo.org
Claroline	http://www.claroline.net
Coggno	http://www.coggno.com
Desire2Learn	http://www.desire2learn.com
Docebo	http://www.docebo.com
Dokeos	http://www.dokeos.com
DyKnow	http://www.dyknow.com
eFront	http://www.efrontlearning.net
Element K	http://www.elementk.com
Evernote	http://www.evernote.com
ExamSoft	http://www.examsoft.com
GlobalScholar	http://www.globalscholar.com
Grockit	http://www.grockit.com

HotChalk	http://www.hotchalk.com
ILIAS	http://www.ilias.de
IMS Global Learning Consortium	http://www.imsglobal.org
Informetica	http://www.informetica.com
Instructure	http://www.instructure.com
JoomlaLMS	http://www.joomlalms.com
Knewton	http://www.knewton.com
Livescribe	http://www.livescribe.com
Moodle	http://www.moodle.org
OLAT	http://www.olat.org
Pluralsight	http://www.pluralsight-training.net
rSmart	http://www.rsmart.com
Saba Software	http://www.saba.com
Sakai	http://www.sakaiproject.org
Sclipo	http://www.sclipo.com
SharePoint LMS	http://www.sharepointlms.com
SMART Technologies	http://www.smarttech.com
SSLearn	http://www.sslearn.com

SumTotal	http://www.sumtotalsystems.com
Tegrity	http://www.tegrity.com
Thinking Cap LMS	http://www.thinkingcap.com
Total Training	http://www.totaltraining.com
Vitalect	http://www.vitalect.com

EMAIL

ActiveCampaign	http://www.activecampaign.com
ClickDimensions	http://www.clickdimensions.com
Electric Mail	http://www.electricmail.com
eM Client	http://www.emclient.com
Exclaimer	http://www.exclaimer.com
Global Relay	http://www.globalrelay.com
Gmail	http://mail.google.com/
Gordano	http://www.gordano.com
Horde	http://www.horde.org
Hotmail	http://www.hotmail.com
IncrediMail	http://www.incredimail.com

Kerio	http://www.kerio.com
LiveOffice	http://www.liveoffice.com
MailChimp	http://www.mailchimp.com
Message Systems	http://www.messagesystems.com
Microsoft Outlook	http://office.microsoft.com/en-us/outlook/
Mimecast	http://www.mimecast.com
Mozilla Thunderbird	http://www.mozillamessaging.com/en-US/thunderbird/
MXSweep	http://www.mxsweep.com
Novell GroupWise	http://www.novell.com/products/groupwise/
Open-Xchange	http://www.open-xchange.com/en/home.html
Postbox	http://www.postbox-inc.com
Proofpoint	http://www.proofpoint.com
Rapportive	http://www.rapportive.com
Roundcube	http://www.roundcube.net
SendGrid	http://www.sendgrid.com
Sendmail	http://www.sendmail.com
Smarsh	http://www.smarsh.com
SMTP.com	http://www.smtp.com

SquirrelMail	http://www.squirrelmail.org
TransVault	http://www.transvault.com
Windows Live Mail	http://explore.live.com/windows-live-mail
Yahoo! Mail	https://login.yahoo.com/
YouSendIt	https://www.yousendit.com
Zimbra	http://www.zimbra.com

ENTREPRENEURSHIP

AllBusiness	http://www.allbusiness.com
Ben Franklin Technology Partners	http://www.benfranklin.org
Capital Factory	http://www.capitalfactory.com
Citrix Startup Accelerator	http://www.citrixstartupaccelerator.com
DEMO	http://www.demo.com
DreamIt Ventures	http://www.dreamitventures.com
Ecorner	http://ecorner.stanford.edu/
Elevator Labs	http://www.elevatorlabs.com
Enloop	http://www.enloop.com
EnterpriseWorks – University of	http://researchpark.illinois.edu/facilities/enterpriseworks/

Illinois	
Entrepreneur	http://www.entrepreneur.com
Enviromental Business Cluster	http://www.environmentalcluster.org
Fast Company	http://www.fastcompany.com
Flashpoint	http://www.flashpointdc.org
FounderFuel	http://www.founderfuel.com/en/
FOX BUSINESS Small Business Center	http://smallbusiness.foxbusiness.com/
General Assembly	http://www.generalassemb.ly
Harvard Business Review	http://www.hbr.org
Inc	http://www.inc.com
LaunchBox Digital	http://www.launchboxdigital.com
Microsoft BizSpark	http://www.microsoft.com/bizspark/
National Collegiate Inventors and Innovators Alliance	http://www.nciia.org
Seedcamp	http://www.seedcamp.com
Small Business Trend	http://www.smallbiztrends.com
SmartMoney	http://www.smartmoney.com
smSmallBusiness	http://www.smsmallbiz.com

Strascheg Center for Entrepreneurship	http://www.sce-web.de
Summer@Highland	http://www.hcp.com/summer/
TechStars	http://www.techstars.org
The Network Journal	http://www.tnj.com
THE WALL STREET JOURNAL Small Business	http://online.wsj.com/small-business/
TiEcon	http://www.tiecon.org
UNIVERSITY CITY SCIENCE CENTER	http://www.sciencecenter.org
Y Combinator	http://www.ycombinator.com
Year One Labs	http://www.yearonelabs.com
YouWeb	http://www.youwebinc.net

EVENTS

Amazon Web Service (AWS) Start-Up Challenge	http://aws.amazon.com/startupchallenge/
BlackBerry Developer Challenge	http://us.blackberry.com/developers/dev_challenge.jsp
Dell Social Innovation Competition	http://www.dellsocialinnovationcompetition.com

Dream Build Play	http://www.dreambuildplay.com
Garage48	http://www.garage48.org
Google Code Jam	http://code.google.com/codejam/
Google I/O	http://www.google.com/io
Imagine Cup	http://www.imaginecup.com
JourneyEd	http://www.journeyed.com
Microsoft Student Lounge	http://www.msstudentlounge.com
Microsoft Student to Business	http://microsoft.com/studentstobusiness/home/default.aspx
RoboCup	http://www.robocup.org
TechCrunch Disrupt	http://disrupt.techcrunch.com/
ThinkQuest	http://www.thinkquest.org/en/

FRAMEWORK

Adobe Flex	http://www.adobe.com/products/flex/
Cappuccino	http://www.cappuccino.org
Catalyst	http://www.catalystframework.org
CherryPy	http://www.cherrypy.org

DooPHP	http://www.doophp.com
Eclipse Communication Framework	http://www.eclipse.org/ecf/
Microsoft .Net	http://www.microsoft.com/net/
Microsoft Sync Framework	http://msdn.microsoft.com/en-us/sync/bb736753
OESIS Framework	http://www.opswat.com/products/oesis-frameworkae/overview
Play Framework	http://www.playframework.org
Ruby on Rails	http://www.rubyonrails.org
Smart GWT	http://code.google.com/p/smartgwt/
Snap Framework	http://snapframework.com
SproutCore	http://www.sproutcore.com
Stripes	http://www.stripesframework.org
Struts	http://struts.apache.org/
Yii	http://www.yiiframework.com
Zend Framework	http://framework.zend.com/

GAME DEVELOPMENT

APP HUB	http://create.msdn.com/en-US/
Atari	http://www.atari.com

CraftyJS	http://www.craftyjs.com
CrowdStar	http://www.crowdstar.com
DroidGamers	http://www.droidgamers.com
Effect Games	http://www.effectgames.com/effect/
Gamasutra	http://www.gamasutra.com
GameDev.Net	http://www.gamedev.net
GameHouse	http://www.gamehouse.com
Games.net	http://www.games.net
Heyzap	http://www.heyzap.com
IGN	http://www.ign.com
ImpactJS	http://wwwimpactjs.com
Joystiq	http://www.joystiq.com
Kiip	http://www.kiip.me
LEGO	http://www.lego.com
LimeJS	http://www.limejs.com
NEXON	http://www.nexon.net
Nintendo	http://www.nintendo.com
OGRE	http://www.ogre3d.org

OnLive	http://www.onlive.com
Playdom	http://www.playdom.com
PlayStation	http://us.playstation.com/
Pogo	http://www.pogo.com
ROBLOX	http://www.roblox.com
RuneScape	http://www.runescape.com
SEGA	http://www.sega.com
Unity 3D	http://www.unity3d.com
We R Interactive	http://www.werinteractive.com
Xbox Developer	http://www.xbox.com/en-US/community/developer/
YoYo Games	http://www.yoyogames.com
ZBrush	http://www.pixologic.com
Zylom	http://www.zylom.com/us/en/

GIS/GPS

Arkon	http://www.arkon.com
Ashtech	http://www.ashtech.com
Blom	http://www.blomasa.com

deCarta	http://www.decarta.com
DeLorme	http://www.delorme.com
EasyGPS	http://www.easygps.com
Ekahau	http://www.ekahau.com
EmerGeo	http://www.emergeo.com
Esri	http://www.esri.com
Fugawi	http://www.fugawi.com
Garmin	http://www.garmin.com
GeoAPI	http://www.geoapi.org
GeoEye	http://www.geoeye.com
GeoTerraImage	http://www.geoterraimage.com
GiSTEQ	http://www.gisteq.com
Google Earth	http://www.google.com/earth/index.html
Groundspeak	http://www.groundspeak.com
Haicom	http://www.haicom.com.tw
HOLUX	http://www.holux.com
INRIX	http://www.inrix.com
Intergraph	http://www.intergraph.com

Leica Geosystems	http://www.leica-geosystems.com
Lowrance	http://www.lowrance.com
Magellan	http://www.magellangps.com
MapFactor	http://www.mapfactor.com/en/
Microsoft UltraCam	http://www.microsoft.com/ultracam/en-us/default.aspx
Mio	http://www.mio.com
NAVIGON	http://www.navigon.com
Navman	http://www.navman.com
Navmii	http://www.navmii.com
NNG	http://www.igomyway.com
Open Geospatial Consortium	http://www.opengeospatial.org
Pharos	http://www.pharosgps.com
Pointools	http://www.pointools.com
PostGIS	http://postgis.refractions.net/
RapidEye	http://www.rapideye.de
SimActive	http://www.simactive.com
Spectra Precision	http://www.spectraprecision.com
Telmap	http://www.telmap.com

TomTom	http://www.tomtom.com
Trimble	http://www.trimble.com
u-blox	http://www.u-blox.com
USGlobalsat	http://www.usglobalsat.com

GRAPHICS AND DESIGNS

3Dconnexion	http://www.3dconnexion.com
3DLabs	http://www.3dlabs.com
3M	http://www.3m.com
Adesso	http://www.adesso.com
Adobe Design Center	http://www.adobe.com/designcenter/
Adobe InDesign	http://www.adobe.com/products/indesign.html
Adode Fireworks	http://www.adobe.com/products/fireworks.html
Agfa Graphics	http://www.agfagraphics.com
Altium	http://www.altium.com
AMD Fusion	http://fusion.amd.com/
ATEN	http://www.aten.com
ATI	http://www.amd.com/us/products/Pages/graphics.aspx

AutoCAD	http://usa.autodesk.com/autocad/
Autodesk	http://usa.autodesk.com/
Autodesk Maya	http://usa.autodesk.com/maya/
AverMedia	http://www.avermedia.com
Bentley Systems	http://www.bentley.com/en-US/
Blender	http://www.blender.org
Clipart.com	http://www.clipart.com
Co.Design	http://www.fastcodesign.com
Connect3D	http://www.connect3d.com
Corel	http://www.corel.com
DAZ 3D	http://www.daz3d.com
Diablotek	http://www.diablotek.com
DrawPlus	http://www.serif.com/drawplus/
Dynamic Graphics	http://www.dynamicgraphics.com
EGVA	http://www.evga.com
Eizo	http://www.eizo.com
Elgato	http://www.elgato.com
EVGA	http://www.evga.com

Foxconn	http://www.foxconn.com
Gefen	http://www.gefen.com
GIGABYTE	http://www.gigabyte.com
GIMP-GNU Image Manipulation Program	http://www.gimp.org
Google SketchUp	http://sketchup.google.com/
Graphics.com	http://www.graphics.com
Hauppauge Computer Works	http://www.hauppauge.com
ImageMagick	http://www.imagemagick.org
Inkd	http://www.inkd.com
Inkscape	http://www.inkscape.org
Intel HD	http://www.intel.com/technology/graphics/intelhd.htm
Irrlicht	http://irrlicht.sourceforge.net/
Logo Works	http://www.logoworks.com
Matrox	http://www.matrox.com
Maxon Computers	http://www.maxon.net
Maxwell Render	http://www.maxwellrender.com
MyDesignShop	http://www.mydesignshop.com

NVIDIA	http://www.nvidia.com
OGRE 3D	http://www.ogre3d.org
OpenGL	http://www.opengl.org
OpenGL ES	http://www.khronos.org/opengles/
OpenSceneGraph	http://www.openscenegraph.org
Panda3D	http://www.panda3d.org
Quark	http://www.quark.com
QuarkXPress	http://www.quark.com/Products/QuarkXPress/
Rotring	http://www.rotring.com
Scalable Vector Graphics (SVG)	http://www.w3.org/Graphics/SVG/
Scribus	http://www.scribus.net
SolidWorks	http://www.solidworks.com
StockLogos	http://www.stocklogos.com
TRITTON	http://www.trittonusa.com
ViewCast	http://www.viewcast.com
VisionTek	http://www.visiontek.com
Wacom	http://www.wacom.com
Zogis	http://www.zogis.com

ZOTAC	http://www.zotacusa.com

GREEN

CleanTech.Org	http://www.cleantech.org
EarthShare	http://www.earthshare.org
ecolife.com	http://www.ecolife.com
EcoPressed	http://www.ecopressed.com
GenGreen	http://www.gengreenlife.com
Go Wireless Go Green	http://www.gowirelessgogreen.org
GreenBiz.com	http://www.greenbiz.com
Jetson Green	http://www.jetsongreen.com
JouleX	http://www.joulex.net
Leafsnap	http://www.leafsnap.com
OnGreen	http://www.ongreen.com
SANYO	http://panasonic.net/sanyo/
SmartPlanet	http://www.smartplanet.com
SolarCity	http://www.solarcity.com
Solaria	http://www.solaria.com

Solyndra	http://www.solyndra.com
SunPower	http://us.sunpowercorp.com
TreeHugger	http://www.treehugger.com
Trees for the Future	http://www.plant-trees.org
Yingli	http://www.yinglisolar.com

HARDWARE DEVELOPMENT

ABB Robots	http://www.abb.com/robots
Aldebaran Robotics	http://www.aldebaran-robotics.com/en
AMX	http://www.amx.com
Anybots	http://www.anybots.com
Arduino	http://www.arduino.cc
Atmel	http://www.atmel.com
Barcoding Inc	http://www.barcoding.com
Bluetooth	http://www.bluetooth.com
CoroWare	http://robotics.coroware.com/
Crestron	http://www.crestron.com
CUDA (Compute Unified	http://www.nvidia.com/object/cuda_home_new.html

Device Architecture)	
DisplayPort	http://www.displayport.org
Emotiv	http://www.emotiv.com
Energid	http://www.energid.com
European Robotics Technology Platform (EUROP)	http://www.robotics-platform.eu
ExpressCard	http://www.usb.org/developers/expresscard
Fairchild Semiconductor	http://www.fairchildsemi.com
Festo	http://www.festo-didactic.com/int-en
Freescale Semiconductor	http://www.freescale.com
Gostai	http://www.gostai.com
HDMI-High Definition Multimedia Interface	http://www.hdmi.org
iRobot	http://www.irobot.com
KUKA Robotics	http://www.kuka-robotics.com/en/
LEGO Mindstorms	http://mindstorms.lego.com/

Lynxmotion	http://www.lynxmotion.com
MakerBot	http://www.makerbot.com
Maxon Motor	http://www.maxonmotor.com
Mentor Graphics	http://www.mentor.com
Microsoft Robotics	http://www.microsoft.com/robotics/
Mobile Robots	http://www.mobilerobots.com
Omek Interactive	http://www.omekinteractive.com
OpenCL	http://www.khronos.org/opencl/
Parallax	http://www.parallax.com
Phidgets	http://www.phidgets.com
RapidRun	http://www.rapidrun.com
Robotics Connection	http://www.roboticsconnection.com
Robotics Trends	http://www.roboticsbusinessreview.com
Shadow Robot	http://www.shadowrobot.com
U3	http://u3.sandisk.com/
Universal Robotics	http://www.universalrobotics.com
URBI – Universal Robot Body Interface	http://www.urbiforge.org

USB – Universal Serial Bus	http://www.usb.org
Wi-Fi Alliance	http://www.wi-fi.org
ZigBee	http://www.zigbee.org

IMAGING

3M	http://www.3m.com
AAXA	http://www.aaxatech.com
Accusoft Pegasus	http://www.accusoft.com
Adobe PostScript	http://www.adobe.com/products/postscript/
AGFA	http://www.agfa.com
Aiptek	http://www.aiptek.com
ARRI	http://www.arri.de
Axis	http://www.axis.com
BenQ	http://www.benq.com
Bodelin	http://www.bodelin.com
Brother	http://www.brother-usa.com
Canon	http://www.canon.com
CardScan	http://www.cardscan.com

CASIO	http://www.casio.com
Christie Digital	http://www.christiedigital.com
Contour	http://www.contour.com
Dell	http://www.dell.com
DXG	http://www.dxgusa.com
DYMO	http://www.dymo.com
EIZO	http://www.eizo.com
Epson	http://www.epson.com
FAVI	http://www.favientertainment.com
Fujifilm	http://www.fujifilm.com
Funai	http://www.funaiworld.com
General Imaging	http://www.general-imaging.com
GoPro	http://www.gopro.com
Hitachi	http://www.hitachi.com
HiTi	http://www.hiti.com/us/
HP	http://www.hp.com
Imation	http://www.imation.com/en-us/
InFocus	http://www.infocus.com

Intova	http://www.intova.net
JVC	http://www.jvc.com
Kodak	http://www.kodak.com
Konica Minolta	http://www.konicaminolta.com
KYOCERA	http://global.kyocera.com/
Leica Camera	http://www.leica-camera.com
Lexmark	http://www.lexmark.com
Lytro	http://www.lytro.com
MAGNAVOX	http://www.magnavox.com
MicroVision	http://www.microvision.com
Monotype Imaging	http://www.monotypeimaging.com
Mustek	http://www.mustek.com
NEC	http://www.nec.com
Nikon	http://www.nikon.com
OKI	http://www.oki.com
Olivetti	http://www.olivetti.com
Olympus	http://www.olympus-global.com/en/
Opteka	http://www.opteka.com

Optoma	http://www.optoma.com
Panasonic	http://www.panasonic.com
PanDigital	http://www.pandigital.net
Pantone	http://www.pantone.com
PENTAX	http://www.pentax.jp/english/
Phillips	http://www.philips.com
Plustek	http://www.plustek.com
Polaroid	http://www.polaroid.com
Ricoh	http://www.ricoh.com
SAMSUNG	http://www.samsung.com
SHARP	http://www.sharp-world.com
Sony	http://www.sony.com
TiVo	http://www.tivo.com
uCorder	http://www.ucorder.com
Uniden	http://www.uniden.com
ViewSonic	http://www.viewsonic.com
Visioneer	http://www.visioneer.com
Vivitar	http://www.vivitar.com

Vivitek	http://www.vivitekcorp.com
VIZIO	http://www.vizio.com
VuPoint	http://www.vupointsolutions.com
Xerox	http://www.xerox.com
Zebra	http://www.zebra.com

INSTANT MESSAGING

Adium	http://www.adium.im
AIM	http://www.aim.com
Apple Facetime	http://www.apple.com/mac/facetime/
BitlBee	http://www.bitlbee.org
BlackBerry Messenger	http://us.blackberry.com/apps-software/blackberrymessenger/
Camfrog	http://www.camfrog.com
eBuddy	http://www.ebuddy.com
Facebook Chat	http://www.facebook.com/sitetour/chat.php
Fetion	http://www.fetion.com.cn
Gadu-Gadu	http://www.gadu-gadu.pl
Gajim	http://www.gajim.org

Google Talk	http://www.google.com/talk/
IBM Sametime	http://www.ibm.com/lotus/sametime
ICQ	http://www.icq.com/en
IMVU	http://www.imvu.com
Jitsi	http://www.jitsi.org
Meebo	http://www.meebo.com
Miranda IM	http://www.miranda-im.org
Mxit	http://www.mxit.com
Nimbuzz	http://www.nimbuzz.com
Olark	http://www.olark.com
Paltalk	http://www.paltalk.com
Pidgin	http://www.pidgin.im
Qnext	http://www.qnext.com
Quassel IRC	http://www.quassel-irc.org
Skype	http://www.skype.com
Softros LAN Messenger	http://messenger.softros.com/
Tencent QQ	http://www.imqq.com
Trillian	http://www.trillian.im

VZOchat	http://www.vzochat.com
Windows Live Messenger	http://explore.live.com/windows-live-messenger
Yahoo! Messenger	http://messenger.yahoo.com/

INTERNET/NETWORK

10ZiG	http://www.10zig.com
Absolute Performance	http://www.absolute-performance.com
ADVA Optical Networking	http://www.advaoptical.com
Anchiva	http://www.anchiva.com
ArcSight	http://www.arcsight.com
Array Networks	http://www.arraynetworks.net
Astaro	http://www.astaro.com
Avenda Systems	http://www.avendasys.com
Axis	http://www.axis.com
Backtrack	http://www.backtrack-linux.org
Barracuda Networks	http://www.barracudanetworks.com
BeyondTrust	http://www.beyondtrust.com
Bivio Networks	http://www.bivio.net

Blue Coat	http://www.bluecoat.com
BlueArc	http://www.bluearc.com
BreakingPoint Systems	http://www.breakingpointsystems.com
Celestix	http://www.celestix.com
CFEngine	http://www.cfengine.com
Check Point	http://www.checkpoint.com
Cisco IronPort	http://www.cisco.com/web/about/ac49/ac0/ac1/ac259/ironport.html
Cloudmark	http://www.cloudmark.com
Commtouch	http://www.commtouch.com
Compellent	http://www.compellent.com
Crossbeam	http://www.crossbeam.com
Cyber-Ark	http://www.cyber-ark.com
Dell SecureWorks	http://www.secureworks.com
eEye Digital Security	http://www.eeye.com
Expand Networks	http://www.expand.com
ExtraHop	http://www.extrahop.com
Extreme Networks	http://www.extremenetworks.com
Fortinet	http://www.fortinet.com

GajShield	http://www.gajshield.com
GFI	http://www.gfi.com
Global DataGuard	http://www.globaldataguard.com
GoToManage	http://www.gotomanage.com
GoToMyPC	http://www.gotomypc.com
H3C	http://www.h3c.com
Infinera	http://www.infinera.com
Infoblox	http://www.infoblox.com
IntelliNet	http://www.intellinet-tech.com
Ipswitch	http://www.ipswitch.com
Kaseya	http://www.kaseya.com
Lancope	http://www.lancope.com
LogLogic	http://www.loglogic.com
LogMeIn	https://secure.logmein.com/
ManageEngine	http://www.manageengine.com
Mellanox	http://www.mellanox.com
Meraki	http://www.meraki.com
Microsoft SharePoint	http://sharepoint.microsoft.com/

Microsoft System Center	http://www.microsoft.com/systemcenter/
Microsoft Windows Server	http://www.microsoft.com/servers/en/us/default.aspx
MikroTik	http://www.mikrotik.com
MSDN Networking Developer Platform Center	http://msdn.microsoft.com/en-us/network/
Nagios	http://www.nagios.org
NetMotion Wireless	http://www.netmotionwireless.com
NetWitness	http://www.netwitness.com
NetWrix	http://www.netwrix.com
Nginx	http://www.nginx.org
Nimsoft	http://www.nimsoft.com
NitroSecurity	http://www.nitrosecurity.com
Node.js	http://www.nodejs.org
Open Compute Project	http://www.opencompute.org
Opengear	http://www.opengear.com
OpenVPN	http://www.openvpn.net

OPNET	http://www.opnet.com
Palo Alto Networks	http://www.paloaltonetworks.com/index.php
pfSense	http://www.pfsense.org
Qosmos	http://www.qosmos.com
Qualys	http://www.qualys.com
Radware	http://www.radware.com
RedSeal	http://www.redseal.net
RSA	http://www.rsa.com
SafeNet	http://www.safenet-inc.com
SANS	http://www.sans.org
Server Density	http://www.serverdensity.com
Skybox Security	http://www.skyboxsecurity.com
SkyRecon	http://www.skyrecon.com
Solar Winds	http://www.solarwinds.com
SolarWinds	http://www.solarwinds.com
SonicWALL	http://www.sonicwall.com/us/
Spiceworks	http://www.spiceworks.com
StillSecure	http://www.stillsecure.com

Stonesoft	http://www.stonesoft.com/en/
Stratus	http://www.stratus.com
Supermicro	http://www.supermicro.com
Transition Networks	http://www.transition.com
Tufin	http://www.tufin.com
VirusTotal	http://www.virustotal.com
WatchGuard	http://www.watchguard.com
Websense	http://www.websense.com
XDE SDK	http://developer.cisco.com/web/xde
Zabbix	http://www.zabbix.com

JAVA DEVELOPMENT

AspectJ	http://www.eclipse.org/aspectj/
BIRT	http://www.eclipse.org/birt/
BlueJ	http://www.bluej.org
Checkstyle	http://checkstyle.sourceforge.net/
DWR- Direct Web Remoting	http://www.directwebremoting.org
Enterprise JavaBeans	http://www.oracle.com/technetwork/java/javaee/ejb/index.html

Technology (EJB)	
Ext GWT	http://www.sencha.com/products/extgwt/
FreeMaker	http://freemarker.sourceforge.net/
Glassfish	http://glassfish.java.net/
Greenfoot	http://www.greenfoot.org
Hibernate	http://www.hibernate.org
JARS	http://www.jars.com
Java Community Process – JCP	http://www.jcp.org
Java ME	http://www.oracle.com/technetwork/java/javame/index.html
Java.net	http://www.java.net
JavaFX	http://www.javafx.com
JavaWorld	http://www.javaworld.com
jGuru	http://www.jguru.com
JNDI – Java Naming and Directory Interface	http://www.oracle.com/technetwork/java/jndi/index.html
LearnNowJava	http://www.learnnowjava.com
OSGi	http://www.osgi.org

PMD	http://pmd.sourceforge.net/
Solr	http://lucene.apache.org/solr/
Spring	http://www.springsource.org
Vaadin	http://www.vaadin.com

LINUX

ALT Linux	http://www.altlinux.com
Arch Linux	http://www.archlinux.org
Calculate Linux	http://www.calculate-linux.org/en
CentOS	http://www.centos.org
Chakra	http://www.chakra-project.org
CrunchBang	http://www.crunchbanglinux.org
Debian	http://www.debian.org
Dreamlinux	http://www.dreamlinux.net
Edubuntu	http://www.edubuntu.org
Fedora	http://www.fedoraproject.org
Gentoo Linux	http://www.gentoo.org
HP Linux Imaging and Printing (HPLIP)	http://www.hplip.net

Linux Foundation	http://www.linuxfoundation.org
Linux Kernel	http://www.kernel.org
Linux Mint	http://www.linuxmint.com
Linux.com	http://www.linux.com
Mageia	http://www.mageia.org
MEPIS	http://www.mepis.org
MontaVista	http://www.mvista.com
openSUSE	http://www.opensuse.org/en/
PCLinuxOS	http://www.pclinuxos.com
Puppy Linux	http://www.puppylinux.org
Red Flag Linux	http://www.redflag-linux.com/en/
Red Hat	http://www.redhat.com
Sabayon	http://www.sabayon.org
Scientific Linux	http://www.scientificlinux.org
Slackware Linux	http://www.slackware.com
SUSE Linux Enterprise	http://www.novell.com/linux/
Ubuntu	http://www.ubuntu.com

MAPS

ArcGIS	http://www.esri.com/software/arcgis/index.html
Bing Maps	http://www.bing.com/maps/
GeoRSS	http://www.georss.org
Google Maps	http://maps.google.com/
Intermap	http://www.intermap.com
MapQuest	http://www.mapquest.com
Mapyx QUO	http://www.mapyx.com
Microsoft MapPoint	http://www.microsoft.com/mappoint/
NAVTEQ	http://www.navteq.com
OpenLayers	http://www.openlayers.org
OpenStreetMap	http://www.openstreetmap.org
Pitney Bowes MapInfo	http://www.pbinsight.com/welcome/mapinfo/
TeleNav	http://www.telenav.com
Yahoo! Maps	http://maps.yahoo.com/

MARKET RESEARCH

451 Group	http://www.451group.com
Aberdeen Group	http://www.aberdeen.com

Asymco	http://www.asymco.com
BeyeNETWORK	http://www.b-eye-network.com
ChangeWave Research	http://www.changewaveresearch.com
comScore	http://www.comscore.com
DCIG	http://www.dcig.com
Distimo	http://www.distimo.com
Enterprise Management Associates	http://www.enterprisemanagement.com
Enterprise Strategy Group	http://www.enterprisestrategygroup.com
Forrester	http://www.forrester.com
Frost & Sullivan	http://www.frost.com
Gartner	http://www.gartner.com
IDC	http://www.idc.com
Nielsen	http://www.nielsen.com
NPD Group	http://www.npd.com
Osterman Research	http://www.ostermanresearch.com
Point Topic	http://www.point-topic.com
SANS	http://www.sans.org

Strategy Analytics	http://www.strategyanalytics.com
Tier1Research	http://www.t1r.com
UBS	http://www.ubs.com
VisionMobile	http://www.visionmobile.com
Wainhouse Reasearch	http://www.wainhouse.com

MATHEMATICS/STATISTICS

Desmos	http://www.desmos.com
Euler Math Toolbox	http://eumat.sourceforge.net/
GNU Octave	http://www.gnu.org/software/octave/
Gnuplot	http://www.gnuplot.info
GSL - GNU Scientific Library	http://www.gnu.org/software/gsl/
LAPACK	http://www.netlib.org/lapack/
Magma Computational Algebra System	http://magma.maths.usyd.edu.au/magma/
Maplesoft Maple	http://www.maplesoft.com/products/maple/
Mathcad	http://www.ptc.com/products/mathcad/
Mathematica	http://www.wolfram.com/mathematica/

Mathomatic	http://www.mathomatic.org/math/
MATLAB	http://www.mathworks.com/products/matlab/
Matplotlib	http://matplotlib.sourceforge.net/
Maxima	http://maxima.sourceforge.net/
Microsoft Math	http://www.microsoft.com/math/default.mspx
Minitab	http://www.minitab.com
Modrian	http://www.rosuda.org/mondrian/
Quid	http://www.quid.com
R	http://www.r-project.org
Sage	http://www.sagemath.org
Singular	http://www.singular.uni-kl.de/
Smath Studio	http://www.smath.info
SPSS	http://www.spss.com
SymPy	http://www.sympy.org
Tulip	http://tulip.labri.fr/TulipDrupal/

MEMORY/STORAGE

3PAR	http://h18006.www1.hp.com/storage/disk_storage/3par/index.html

Adaptec	http://www.adaptec.com
ADATA	http://www.adatausa.com
Addonics	http://www.addonics.com
Adtron	http://www.adtron.com
Amazon S3	http://aws.amazon.com/s3/
Atarza	http://www.atarza.com
BridgeSTOR	http://www.bridgestor.com
Buffalo Technology	http://www.buffalotech.com
Buslink	http://www.buslink.com
CommVault	http://www.commvault.com
Coraid	http://www.coraid.com
Corsair	http://www.corsair.com
Crucial	http://www.crucial.com
Data Domain	http://www.datadomain.com
Dataram	http://www.dataram.com
Delkin Devices	http://www.delkin.com
Diskeeper	http://www.diskeeper.com
Drobo	http://www.drobo.com

Eee STORAGE	http://www.eeestorage.com
Emulex	http://www.emulex.com
FalconStor	http://www.falconstor.com
Fujitsu	http://www.fujitsu.com
HighPoint	http://www.highpoint-tech.com
IBM Storage	http://www.ibm.com/servers/storage/index.html
Imation	http://www.imation.com
Intel Thunderbolt	http://www.intel.com/technology/io/thunderbolt/index.htm
Iomega	http://www.iomega.com
ioSafe	http://www.iosafe.com
Kanguru	https://www.kanguru.com
Kingston	http://www.kingston.com
LaCie	http://www.lacie.com
Lexar	http://www.lexar.com
Lite-On	http://www.liteon.com
LSI	http://www.lsi.com
Memorex	http://www.memorex.com/en-us/
Memoright	http://www.memoright.com

Micron	http://www.micron.com
Mushkin	http://www.mushkin.com
NEC	http://www.nec.com
NewerTech	http://www.newertech.com
Nexsan	http://www.nexsan.com
Nimble Storage	http://www.nimblestorage.com
OCZ Technology	http://www.ocztechnology.com
Patriot Memory	http://www.patriotmemory.com
Plextor	http://www.plextor.com
PNY	http://www.pny.com
PRETEC	http://www.pretec.com
Pure Storage	http://www.purestorage.com
QNAP	http://www.qnap.com
Rambus	http://www.rambus.com/us/
Rimage	http://www.rimage.com
Rocstor	http://www.rocstor.com
RunCore	http://www.runcore.com
SandForce	http://www.sandforce.com

SanDisk	http://www.sandisk.com
Sans Digital	http://www.sansdigital.com
Seagate	http://www.seagate.com
Spectra Logic	http://www.spectralogic.com
StorageCraft	http://www.storagecraft.com
Super Talent	http://www.supertalent.com
Supermicro	http://www.supermicro.com
Synology	http://www.synology.com
TEAC	http://www.teac.com
Toshiba	http://www.toshiba.com
Transcend	http://www.transcendusa.com
Traxdata	http://www.traxdata.com
Vantec	http://www.vantecusa.com
Verbatim	http://www.verbatim.com
Virsto	http://www.virsto.com
Western Digital	http://www.wdc.com
Xiotech	http://www.xiotech.com
YuuWaa	http://www.yuuwaa.com

MOBILE TECHNOLOGY

3rd Generation Partnership Project – 3GPP	http://www.3gpp.org
Acision	http://www.acision.com
Airpush	http://www.airpush.com
Android	http://www.android.com
Android Central	http://www.androidcentral.com
AndroidZoom	http://www.androidzoom.com
Angström	http://www.angstrom-distribution.org
Appcelerator	http://www.appcelerator.com
Arkon	http://www.arkon.com
Bada	http://www.bada.com
BBGeeks	http://www.bbgeeks.com
BerryReview	http://www.berryreview.com
BlueStacks	http://www.bluestacks.com
BlueVia	http://www.bluevia.com
Brew MP	http://www.brewmp.com
Canvas	http://www.gocanvas.com
Clickatell	http://www.clickatell.com

CrackBerry	http://www.crackberry.com
DeviceAnywhere	http://www.deviceanywhere.com
Digby	http://www.digby.com
EA Mobile	http://www.eamobile.com
eyeSight	http://www.eyesight-tech.com
FlipBoard	http://www.flipboard.com
Flurry	http://www.flurry.com
FrontlineSMS	http://www.frontlinesms.com
FunMobility	http://www.funmobility.com
GetJar	http://www.getjar.com
GroupMe	http://www.groupme.com
GSM World	http://www.gsmworld.com
Handango	http://www.handango.com
HeyWire	http://www.heywire.com
Intermec	http://www.intermec.com
Intrinsyc	http://www.intrinsyc.com
Kno	http://www.kno.com
Layar	http://www.layar.com

Maemo	http://www.maemo.org
Medialets	http://www.medialets.com
MediaTek	http://www.mediatek.com
MeeGo	http://www.meego.com
Millennial Media	http://www.millennialmedia.com
Mob4Hire	http://www.mob4hire.com
Mobify	http://www.mobify.me
MobiHand	http://www.mobihand.com
MobileApps.com	http://www.mobileapps.com
MobileCrunch	http://www.mobilecrunch.com
mobileFX	http://www.mobilefx.com
Mobipocket	http://www.mobipocket.com
MobiTV	http://www.mobitv.com
MonoTouch	http://www.monotouch.net
Motricity	http://www.motricity.com
Nearbuy Systems	http://www.nearbuysystems.com
NeuStar	http://www.neustar.biz
Nokia Experts	http://www.nokiaexperts.com

Notifo	http://www.notifo.com
OnSwipe	http://www.onswipe.com
Open Handset Alliance	http://www.openhandsetalliance.com
OpenEmbedded	http://www.openembedded.org
OpenPlug	http://www.openplug.com
Opinionaided	http://www.opinionaided.com
Ovi	http://www.ovi.com
Palm Developer	http://developer.palm.com/
Paperlinks	http://www.paperlinks.com
PhoneGap	http://www.phonegap.com
PocketGear	http://www.pocketgear.com
PreCentral	http://www.precentral.net
Qt	http://qt.nokia.com/products/
Sencha Touch	http://www.sencha.com/products/touch/
Sierra Wireless	http://www.sierrawireless.com
SlideME	http://www.slideme.org
Smith Micro	http://www.smithmicro.com
SOTI	http://www.soti.net

StackMob	http://www.stackmob.com
ST-ERICSSON	http://www.stericsson.com
Symbian	http://symbian.nokia.com/
TiPb	http://www.tipb.com
TreoCentral	http://www.treocentral.com
Urban Airship	http://www.urbanairship.com
VisualOn	http://www.visualon.com
Windows Embedded	http://msdn.microsoft.com/embedded/
Windows Mobile	http://microsoft.com/windowsmobile/
Windows Phone	http://www.microsoft.com/windowsphone
WPCentral	http://www.wpcentral.com

MODELING

Agile Alliance	http://www.agilealliance.org
Agile Modeling	http://www.agilemodeling.com
ArgoUML	http://argouml.tigris.org/
BPMN – Business Process Modeling Notation	http://www.bpmn.org
Cadence Design Systems	http://www.cadence.com

CMMI – Capability Maturity Model Integration	http://www.sei.cmu.edu/cmmi/
Common Object Request Broker Architecture (CORBA)	http://www.corba.org
Google SketchUp	http://sketchup.google.com/
Microsoft Visio	http://office.microsoft.com/en-us/visio/
Object Management Group (OMG)	http://www.omg.org
OMG Model Driven Architecture	http://www.omg.org/mda
Sparx Systems	http://www.sparxsystems.com.au
StarUML	http://staruml.sourceforge.net/en/
Unified Modeling Language (UML)	http://www.uml.org

NEWS

ACM XRDS	http://xrds.acm.org/
Advisor	http://www.advisor.com
AllThingsD	http://www.allthingsd.com
Business Insider	http://www.businessinsider.com
Campus Technology	http://www.campustechnology.com
cellular-news	http://www.cellular-news.com

Channel Insider	http://www.channelinsider.com
CIO	http://www.cio.com
Computer Shopper	http://www.computershopper.com
ComputerWorld	http://www.computerworld.com
CRN	http://www.crn.com
CrunchGear	http://www.crunchgear.com
Database Journal	http://www.databasejournal.com
Directions Magazine	http://www.directionsmag.com
Discovery	http://www.discovery.com
DotNetSlackers	http://www.dotnetslackers.com/
Engadget	http://www.engadget.com
eSchool News	http://www.eschoolnews.com
eWeek	http://www.eweek.com
ExtremeTech	http://www.extremetech.com
Geoinformatics.com	http://www.geoinformatics.com
GigaOM	http://www.gigaom.com
GISCafe	http://www.giscafe.com
InformationWeek	http://www.informationweek.com

InfoStor	http://www.infostor.com
InfoWorld	http://www.infoworld.com
Inside Social Games	http://www.insidesocialgames.com
IntoMobile	http://www.intomobile.com
Linux Journal	http://www.linuxjournal.com
LinuxInsider	http://www.linuxinsider.com
Mashable	http://www.mashable.com
Maximum PC	http://www.maximumpc.com
MobiHealthNews	http://www.mobihealthnews.com
MOBILE TECH TODAY	http://www.mobile-tech-today.com
MobileHealthNews	http://www.mobihealthnews.com
O'Reilly Radar	http://radar.oreilly.com/
PC Magazine	http://www.pcmag.com
Practical eCommerce	http://www.practicalecommerce.com
ReadWriteWeb	http://www.readwriteweb.com
Robots.net	http://www.robots.net
SitePoint	http://www.sitepoint.com
Slashdot	http://www.slashdot.org

SmartBrief	http://www.smartbrief.com
SmartComputing	http://www.smartcomputing.com
Smashing Magazine	http://www.smashingmagazine.com
SYS-CON	http://www.sys-con.com
TechCrunch	http://www.techcrunch.com
Techmeme	http://www.techmeme.com
The Next Web	http://www.thenextweb.com
Tom's Hardware	http://www.tomshardware.com
VentureBeat	http://venturebeat.com
Wired	http://www.wired.com
ZDNet	http://www.zdnet.com

ONLINE RESOURCES

Agora	http://www.aginternetwork.org/en/
ASP.NET Videos	http://www.asp.net/learn
Bentham Open E-Journals	http://www.benthamscience.com/open/
Books24x7	http://www.books24x7.com
CareerCast	http://www.careercast.com

Channel 9	http://channel9.msdn.com/
Database Journal	http://www.databasejournal.com
Dev Articles	http://www.devarticles.com
eJDS	http://library.ictp.it/ejds
Electronic Journal of Biotechnology	http://www.ejbiotechnology.info
Electronic Journal of Information Systems Evaluation	http://www.ejise.com
FAQs.org	http://www.faqs.org
HCI Bibliography	http://www.hcibib.org
HighWire	http://highwire.stanford.edu/
Hindawi Journals	http://www.hindawi.com/journals/
INASP	http://www.inasp.info
Issuu	http://www.issuu.com
JSTOR	http://www.jstor.org
Kaye & Laby	http://www.kayelaby.npl.co.uk/
LearnDevNow.com	http://www.learndevnow.com
Library Journal	http://www.libraryjournal.com
MentorNet	http://www.mentornet.net

Microwave Journal	http://www.mwjournal.com
MSDN	http://msdn.microsoft.com/
OnePetro	http://www.onepetro.org
OPEN Forum	http://www.openforum.com
Oxford Journals	http://www.oxfordjournals.org
Questia	http://www.questia.com
RFID Journal	http://www.rfidjournal.com
Safari Books Online	http://www.safaribooksonline.com
SAGE Publication	http://www.sagepub.com
SpringerLink	http://www.springerlink.com
W3Schools	http://www.w3schools.com
Web Buyer's Guide	http://www.webbuyersguide.com

OPEN SOURCE

Bedework	http://www.bedework.org
Bonjour	http://www.apple.com/bonjour
Git	http://git-scm.com/
JBoss	http://www.jboss.org

Joget Workflow	http://www.joget.org
Longsight	http://www.longsight.com
Mifos	http://www.mifos.org
Open Source Geospatial Foundation (OSGeo)	http://www.osgeo.org
Open Source Initiative	http://www.opensource.org
OpenAjax	http://www.openajax.org
Openbravo	http://www.openbravo.com
OpenLogic	http://www.openlogic.com
OpenNebula.org	http://www.opennebula.org
OpenPetra	http://www.openpetra.org
OpenShift	http://openshift.redhat.com/
Puppet	http://www.puppetlabs.com
Redis	http://www.redis.io

OPERATING SYSTEM

Android	http://www.android.com
Apple iOS	http://www.apple.com/ios
Apple Mac OS X	http://www.apple.com/macosx/

ClearOS	http://www.clearfoundation.com/Software/overview.html
EasyPeasy	http://www.geteasypeasy.com
eComStation	http://www.ecomstation.com
FreeBSD	http://www.freebsd.org
GNOME	http://www.gnome.org
GNU	http://www.gnu.org
Haiku	http://www.haiku-os.org
HP OpenVMS	http://www.hp.com/go/openvms
IBM AIX	http://www.ibm.com/aix
Junos Network Operating System	http://www.juniper.net/us/en/products-services/nos/junos/
Linux	http://www.kernel.org
Microsoft Windows	http://www.microsoft.com/windows/
MikroTik RouterOS	http://www.mikrotik.com/software.html
MINIX 3	http://www.minix3.org
NetBSD	http://www.netbsd.org
OpenBSD	http://www.openbsd.org
Oracle Solaris	http://www.oracle.com/us/solaris/index.html

PC-BSD	http://www.pcbsd.org
QNX	http://www.qnx.com
ReactOS	http://www.reactos.org
Samba	http://www.samba.org
Syllable	http://web.syllable.org/pages/index.html
True64 UNIX	http://h30097.www3.hp.com/
UNIX	http://www.unix.org

ORGANIZATIONS

ACM - Association for Computing Machinery	http://www.acm.org
AIIM	http://www.aiim.org
American Society for Training & Development (ASTD)	http://www.astd.org
ANSI – American National Standards Institute	http://www.ansi.org
APSstandard.org	http://www.apsstandard.org
ASME – American Society of Mechanical Engineers	http://www.asme.org
BCS – British Computer Society	http://www.bcs.org

CDMA Development Group (CDG)	http://www.cdg.org
CTIA	http://www.ctia.org
DLNA – Digital Living Network Alliance	http://www.dlna.org
Ecma Intermational	http://www.ecma-international.org
Ethernet Alliance	http://www.ethernetalliance.org
European Telecommunications Standards Institute – ETSI	http://www.etsi.org
Global Certification Forum - GCF	http://www.globalcertificationforum.org
ICANN - Internet Corporation For Assigned Names and Numbers	http://www.icann.org
IEEE	http://www.ieee.org
IEEE Communications Society	http://www.comsoc.org
IEEE- Computational Intelligence Society	http://www.ieee-cis.org
IEEE Robotics & Automation Society	http://www.ieee-ras.org
IETF – Internet Engineering Task Force	http://www.ietf.org
IFIP – International Federation for Information Processing	http://www.ifip.org

Intellect	http://www.intellectuk.org
International Association of Managed Service Providers	http://www.mspalliance.com
International Function Point User Group – IFPUG	http://www.ifpug.org
International Institute of Business Analysis – IIBA	http://www.iiba.org
International Multimedia Telecommunications Consortium – IMTC	http://www.imtc.org
International Statistical Institute (ISI)	http://www.isi-web.org
International Telecommunication Union – ITU	http://www.itu.int
Internet Engineering Task Force – IETF	http://www.ietf.org
Internet Society	http://www.isoc.org
ISACA - Information Systems Audit and Control Association	http://www.isaca.org
ISES – International Solar Energy Society	http://www.ises.org
ISO-International Organization for Standardization	http://www.iso.org
IT Governance Institute – ITGI	http://www.itgi.org

ITU – International Telecommunication Union	http://www.itu.int
Khronos	http://www.khronos.org
Messaging Anti-Abuse Working Group – MAAWG	http://www.maawg.org
National Collegiate Inventors and Innovators Alliance	http://www.nciia.org
OASIS	http://www.oasis-open.org
Open Group	http://www.opengroup.org
OSGi	http://www.osgi.org
Project Management Institute – PMI	http://www.pmi.org
Software & Information Industry Association – SIIA	http://www.siia.net
THE GREEN GRID	http://www.thegreengrid.org
UL	http://www.ul.com
Unicode	http://www.unicode.org
United Nations (UN)	http://www.un.org
VESA	http://www.vesa.org
WiMAX Forum	http://www.wimaxforum.org

WIPO - World Intellectual Property Organization	http://www.wipo.int
World Information Technology and Services Alliance – WITSA	http://www.witsa.org

PHONES

Acer	http://www.acer.com
Apple	http://www.apple.com
BlackBerry	http://www.blackberry.com
Boost Mobile	http://www.boostmobile.com
Garmin-Asus	http://www.garminasus.com
Haier	http://www.haier.net/index.htm
HTC	http://www.htc.com
KYOCERA	http://global.kyocera.com/
LG	http://www.lge.com
Motorola	http://www.motorola.com
Nokia	http://www.nokia.com
Nokia for Business	http://www.nokiaforbusiness.com
Pantech	http://www.pantechusa.com

Pharos	http://www.pharosgps.com
SAMSUNG	http://www.samsung.com
Siemens	http://www.siemens.com
Sony Ericsson	http://www.sonyericsson.com
Vodafone	http://www.vodafone.com
Vtech	http://www.vtech.com
ZTE	http://wwwen.zte.com.cn/en/

PHOTOGRAPHY

Acratech	http://www.acratech.net
Adobe Photoshop	http://www.adobe.com/products/photoshop.html
Adorama	http://www.adorama.com
Apple Aperture	http://www.apple.com/aperture/
ArcSoft	http://www.arcsoft.com
Corel PaintShop Photo Pro	http://www.corel.com/servlet/Satellite/us/en/Product/1184951547051
DeluxGear	http://www.deluxgear.com
Flickr	http://www.flickr.com
Getty Images	http://www.gettyimages.com

Gitzo	http://www.gitzo.com
Induro	http://www.indurogear.com
Lowepro	http://www.lowepro.com
Manfrotto	http://www.manfrotto.com
OmniVision	http://www.ovt.com
Phase One	http://www.phaseone.com
Photojojo	http://www.photojojo.com
PhotoPlus	http://www.serif.com/photoplus/
Photoscape	http://www.photoscape.org
Picasa	http://picasa.google.com/
PicPlum	https://www.picplum.com
Picwing	http://www.picwing.com
RadioPopper	http://www.radiopopper.com
Snapjoy	http://www.snapjoy.com
Snapsort	http://www.snapsort.com
Tiffen	http://www.tiffen.com
Xara	http://www.xara.com

PHP

CakePHP	http://www.cakephp.org
CodeIgniter	http://www.codeigniter.com
EasyPHP	http://www.easyphp.org
Eclipse PHP Developer Tool	http://www.eclipse.org/pdt/
JetBrains PhpStorm	http://www.jetbrains.com/phpstorm/index.html
PHP	http://www.php.net
PHP on Windows	http://microsoft.com/web/platform/phponwindows.aspx
phpBB	http://www.phpbb.com
PHPEclipse	http://www.phpeclipse.com
PHPList	http://www.phplist.com
phpMyAdmin	http://www.phpmyadmin.net
phpMyDirectory	http://www.phpmydirectory.com
phpPgAdmin	http://phppgadmin.sourceforge.net/
phpsh	http://www.phpsh.org
Smarty	http://www.smarty.net
Symfony	http://www.symfony.com
Twig	http://www.twig-project.org

Xdebug	http://www.xdebug.org
Zend	http://www.zend.com

POWER

Active Power	http://www.activepower.com
Antec	http://www.antec.com
APC	http://www.apc.com
BELKIN	http://www.belkin.com
Cummins	http://www.cummins.com
CyberPower	http://www.cyberpowersystems.com
Duracell	http://www.duracell.com/en-US/index.jspx
Eaton	http://www.eaton.com
Eltek Valere	http://www.eltekvalere.com
Emerson Network Power	http://www.emersonnetworkpower.com
General Electric	http://www.ge.com
Lenmar	http://www.lenmar.com
Maruson	http://www.marusonusa.com
Maxell	http://www.maxell.com

OPTI-UPS	http://www.opti-ups.com
Paradise Datacom	http://www.paradisedata.com
Protection Technology Group	http://www.protectiongroup.com
Schneider Electric	http://www.schneider-electric.com
Siemens	http://www.siemens.com
Sollatek	http://www.sollatek.com
Tripp Lite	http://www.tripplite.com
Uniross	http://www.uniross.com
Verdiem	http://www.verdiem.com

PROCESSORS

Acer	http://www.acer.com
AMD	http://www.amd.com
Asus	http://www.asus.com
Axiom Memory Solutions	http://www.axiommemory.com
Cavium	http://www.cavium.com
Fujitsu	http://www.fujitsu.com
HP	http://www.hp.com

IBM	http://www.ibm.com
Intel	http://www.intel.com
Kingston Technology	http://www.kingston.com
Lenovo	http://www.lenovo.com
NEC Corporation	http://www.nec.com
Newer Technology	http://www.newertech.com
PMC-Sierra	http://www.pmc-sierra.com
Silicon Integrated Systems	http://www.sis.com
Sonnet Technologies	http://www.sonnettech.com
Tilera	http://www.tilera.com
Toshiba	http://www.toshiba.com

PROGRAMMING

Adobe ActionScript	http://www.adobe.com/devnet/actionscript.html
Amzi!	http://www.amzi.com
Microsft Visual Basic	http://msdn.microsoft.com/en-us/vbasic
Tcl – Tool Command Language	http://www.tcl.tk
Cocoa	http://developer.apple.com/technologies/mac/cocoa.html

Erlang	http://www.erlang.org
Microsoft Visual C++	http://msdn.microsoft.com/en-us/visualc/aa336395
NetCOBOL	http://www.netcobol.com
Objective C	http://developer.apple.com/documentation/Cocoa/Conceptual/ObjectiveC/
ActiveState	http://www.activestate.com
Ada Information Clearinghouse	http://www.adaic.org
Charm++	http://charm.cs.uiuc.edu/
Clojure	http://www.clojure.org
Falcon	http://www.falconpl.org
Go	http://www.golang.org
Groovy	http://groovy.codehaus.org/
Haskell	http://www.haskell.org
haXe	http://www.haxe.org
Intel Threaded Building Blocks	http://www.threadingbuildingblocks.org
JRuby	http://www.jruby.org
Logtalk	http://www.logtalk.org

Lua	http://www.lua.org
Microsoft F#	http://www.fsharp.net
Nu Programming Language	http://www.programming.nu
Perl	http://www.perl.org
Pharo	http://www.pharo-project.org/home
Processing	http://www.processing.org
PyGTK	http://www.pygtk.org
Python	http://www.python.org
Rubinius	http://www.rubini.us
Ruby	http://www.ruby-lang.org
Ruby on Rails	http://www.rubyonrails.org
Scratch	http://scratch.mit.edu/
Small Basic	http://msdn.microsoft.com/en-us/ff384126.aspx
Squeak	http://www.squeak.org
wxPython	http://www.wxpython.org

SOCIAL

Acquia	http://www.acquia.com

AddThis	http://www.addthis.com
Adloopz	http://www.adloopz.com
Banckle	http://www.banckle.com
BranchOut	http://www.branchout.com
Claritics	http://www.claritics.com
ClearSpring	http://www.clearspring.com
Delicious	http://www.delicious.com
Designmoo	http://www.designmoo.com
Dribbble	http://www.dribbble.com
Elgg	http://www.elgg.org
ePals	http://www.epals.com
Facebook	http://www.facebook.com
Flickr	http://www.flickr.com
foursquare	https://foursquare.com/
FriendFeed	http://www.friendfeed.com
Gigya	http://www.gigya.com
GitHub	https://www.github.com
GoodReads	http://www.goodreads.com

Google+	https://plus.google.com/
Gowalla	http://www.gowalla.com
hi5	http://www.hi5.com
HootSuite	http://www.hootsuite.com
IMVU	http://www.imvu.com
Jive Software	http://www.jivesoftware.com
LibraryThing	http://www.librarything.com
LinkedIn	http://www.linkedin.com
Meetup	http://www.meetup.com
Myspace	http://www.myspace.com
Ning	http://www.ning.com
Ninua	http://www.ninua.com
OpenSocial	http://www.opensocial.org
Orkut	http://www.orkut.com
Plancast	http://www.plancast.com
Postling	http://www.postling.com
Shareaholic	http://www.shareaholic.com
ShareThis	http://www.sharethis.com

Shelfari	http://www.shelfari.com
Shutterfly	http://www.shutterfly.com
SocialGO	http://www.socialgo.com
Socialspring	http://www.socialspring.com
SocialTimes	http://www.socialtimes.com
StumbleUpon	http://www.stumbleupon.com
Technorati	http://www.technorati.com
Tibbr	http://www.tibbr.com
Twitter	http://www.twitter.com
weRead	http://www.weread.com
Yammer	https://www.yammer.com
Yelp	http://www.yelp.com
Zynga	http://www.zynga.com

SWITCH/ROUTER

ADTRAN	http://www.adtran.com
Allied Telesis	http://www.alliedtelesis.com
Arista Networks	http://www.aristanetworks.com

Asante	http://www.asante.com
Cisco	http://www.cisco.com
D-Link	http://www.dlink.com
Enterasys	http://www.enterasys.com
HP Networking	http://h17007.www1.hp.com/us/en/
IOGEAR	http://www.iogear.com
Juniper Networks	http://www.juniper.net
Marvell	http://www.marvell.com
Mellanox	http://www.mellanox.com
NETGEAR	http://www.netgear.com
Omnitron Systems	http://www.omnitron-systems.com
SMC	http://www.smc.com
TP-LINK	http://www.tp-link.com
TRENDnet	http://www.trendnet.com
ZyXEL	http://www.zyxel.com

SYSTEM TOOLS

7Zip	http://www.7-zip.org

AbiWord	http://www.abisource.com
Ademero	http://www.ademero.com
Adobe Flash Player	http://get.adobe.com/flashplayer/
Adobe InDesign	http://www.adobe.com/products/indesign.html
Adobe Reader	http://get.adobe.com/reader/
AlbumPlus	http://www.serif.com/albumplus/
Animoto	http://www.animoto.com
Apple iTunes	http://www.apple.com/itunes/download/
Apple QuickTime	http://www.apple.com/quicktime/download/
ArcSoft	http://www.arcsoft.com
Ardour	http://www.ardour.org
Ashampoo	http://www.ashampoo.com
Audacity	http://audacity.sourceforge.net/
Aunsoft	http://www.aunsoft.com
Avanquest	http://www.avanquest.com
BlazeVideo	http://www.blazevideo.com
Bluebeam	http://www.bluebeam.com
CCleaner	http://www.piriform.com/ccleaner

CNET TechTracker	http://www.cnet.com/techtracker-free/
CyberLink	http://www.cyberlink.com
Defraggler	http://www.piriform.com/defraggler
DivX	http://www.divx.com
DocuSign	http://www.docusign.com
Druva	http://www.druva.com
Faronics	http://www.faronics.com
Fluxbox	http://www.fluxbox.org
Free Download Manager	http://www.freedownloadmanager.org
Geek Squad	http://www.geeksquad.com
Geekatoo	http://www.geekatoo.com
GOM Software	http://www.gomlab.com
Google Docs	http://docs.google.com/
HP MagCloud	http://www.magcloud.com
ImTOO	http://www.imtoo.com
Internet Download Manager	http://www.internetdownloadmanager.com
IObit	http://www.iobit.com

JetAudio	http://www.jetaudio.com
Kantaris	http://www.kantaris.org
LibreOffice	http://www.libreoffice.org
LightScribe	http://www.lightscribe.com
MagicISO	http://www.magiciso.com
Martview	http://www.martview.com
Microsoft Fix It	http://support.microsoft.com/fixit/
Microsoft Office	http://office.microsoft.com/en-us/
Microsoft Office 365	http://www.microsoft.com/office365/
Microsoft Publisher	http://office.microsoft.com/en-us/publisher/
Microsoft Visio	http://office.microsoft.com/en-us/visio/
Microsoft Windows Media Player	http://windows.microsoft.com/en-US/windows/products/windows-media-player
Miro	http://www.getmiro.com
Nero	http://www.nero.com/eng/
Nitro PDF	http://www.nitropdf.com
OpenOffice	http://www.openoffice.org
Orbit Downloader	http://www.orbitdownloader.com

PagePlus	http://www.serif.com/pageplus/
PC Tools	http://www.pctools.com
PDF Suite	http://www.pdf-suite.com
PhotoPeach	http://www.photopeach.com
Picasa Web Album	https://picasaweb.google.com/home
Picnik	http://www.picnik.com
PKZIP	http://www.pkware.com/software/pkzip/
Power Archiver	http://www.powerarchiver.com
PowerISO	http://www.poweriso.com
PresentationPro	http://www.presentationpro.com
Prevalent Software	http://www.prevasoft.com
PrimoPDF	http://www.primopdf.com
Print Artist	http://www.printartist.com
RARLAB	http://www.rarlab.com
RealPlayer	http://www.real.com
Recuva	http://www.piriform.com/recuva
Roxio	http://www.roxio.com
Runtime Software	http://www.runtime.org

Smith Micro	http://www.smithmicro.com
Soda PDF	http://www.sodapdf.com
SpreadsheetGear	http://www.spreadsheetgear.com
UMPlayer – Universal Media Player	http://www.umplayer.com
VideoLAN	http://www.videolan.org/vlc/
VirtualLab	http://www.binarybiz.com
WavePad	http://www.nch.com.au/wavepad/
Wavosaur	http://www.wavosaur.com
Winamp	http://www.winamp.com
WinZip	http://www.winzip.com
Zune Software	http://www.zune.net/en-us/products/software

TABLET/E-READER

Acer	http://www.acer.com
Aluratek	http://www.aluratek.com
Amazon Kindle	http://www.amazon.com
Apple iPad	http://www.apple.com/ipad/
ARCHOS	http://www.archos.com

ASUS	http://www.asus.com
Barnes&Noble.com Nook	http://www.barnesandnoble.com/nook/index.asp
Coby	http://www.cobyusa.com
Dell	http://www.dell.com
E Ink	http://www.eink.com
ECTACO	http://www.ectaco.com
eLocity	http://www.elocitynow.com
enTourage Systems	http://www.entourageedge.com
Franklin Electronic Publishers	http://www.franklin.com
HP	http://www.hp.com
iriver	http://www.iriver.com
Kobo	http://www.kobobooks.com
KWorld	http://www.kworld-global.com
Lenovo	http://www.lenovo.com
LG	http://www.lge.com
Motion Computing	http://www.motioncomputing.com
Motorola	http://www.motorola.com

MSI	http://www.msi.com
Pandigital	http://www.pandigital.net
Samsung	http://www.samsung.com
Sony	http://www.sony.com
Sungale	http://www.sungale.com
Toshiba	http://www.toshiba.com
Velocity Micro	http://www.velocitymicro.com
ViewSonic	http://www.viewsonic.com
VIZIO	http://www.vizio.com

TELECOMMUNICATION

4RF	http://www.4rf.com
AlanDick	http://www.alandick.com
Astellia	http://www.astellia.com
CellAntenna	http://www.cellantenna.com
Cerillion	http://www.cerillion.com
Comfone	http://www.comfone.com
CommScope	http://www.commscope.com

Comtech EF Data	http://www.comtechefdata.com
DETECON	http://www.detecon.com
Dialogic	http://www.dialogic.com
Evolving Systems	http://www.evolving.com
Harris Corporation	http://www.harris.com
Huawei	http://www.huawei.com
Nomadix	http://www.nomadix.com
Orga Systems	http://www.orga-systems.com
RadiSys	http://www.radisys.com
Redknee	http://www.redknee.com
SkyVision	http://www.skyvision.net
SoftBank	http://www.softbank.co.jp/en/
Telcordia	http://www.telcordia.com
Telenity	http://www.telenity.com
Tellumat	http://www.tellumat.com
ViaSat	http://www.viasat.com
ZTE	http://www.zte.com.cn

UTILITIES

About	http://www.about.com
AccuWeather.com	http://www.accuweather.com
Answers.com	http://www.answers.com
AppData	http://www.appdata.com
Ask	http://www.ask.com
Babylon	http://www.babylon.com
Bing	http://www.bing.com
COLOURlovers	http://www.colourlovers.com
Developer Web Links	http://www.developerweblinks.com
Dictionary.com	http://dictionary.reference.com/
eHow	http://www.ehow.com
GO.com	http://www.go.com
Google	http://www.google.com
GoPollGo	http://www.gopollgo.com
HowStuffWorks	http://www.howstuffworks.com
Instructables	http://www.instructables.com
Kibin	http://www.kibin.com

Name.com	http://www.name.com
Plaxo	http://www.plaxo.com
The Weather Channel	http://www.weather.com
Time and Date	http://www.timeanddate.com
Vizibility	http://www.vizibility.com
Webometrics.info	http://www.webometrics.info
Webopedia	http://www.webopedia.com
Whatis	http://whatis.techtarget.com/
Wikipedia	http://www.wikipedia.org
Wordnik	http://www.wordnik.com

VIDEO

Adobe Premiere	http://www.adobe.com/products/premiere.html
Animoto	http://www.animoto.com
AOL Video	http://video.aol.com/
Auralink	http://www.auralink.com
Automatic Sync	http://www.automaticsync.com
Avid	http://www.avid.com

AVI-SPL	http://www.avispl.com
Boxee	http://www.boxee.tv
Brightcove	http://www.brightcove.com
Caption Colorado	http://www.captioncolorado.com
Celtx	http://www.celtx.com
Cenero	http://www.cenero.com
CPC Closed Captioning	http://www.cpcweb.com
DivX	http://www.divx.com
Docsoft	http://www.docsoft.com
Echo360	http://www.echo360.com
Flowplayer	http://www.flowplayer.org
Glowpoint	http://www.glowpoint.com
Google TV	http://www.google.com/tv/
Kantar Video	http://www.kantarvideo.com
LifeSize	http://www.lifesize.com
Movieclips	http://www.movieclips.com
MoviePlus	http://www.serif.com/movieplus/
MovieStorm	http://www.moviestorm.co.uk

muvee	http://www.muvee.com/en/
Netflix	http://www.netflix.com
Ooyala	http://www.ooyala.com
Panopto	http://www.panopto.com
Pinnacle Systems	http://www.pinnaclesys.com
Polycom	http://www.polycom.com
Qumu	http://www.qumu.com
RealNetworks	http://www.realnetworks.com
ReelSurfer	http://www.reelsurfer.com
RipCode	http://www.ripcode.com
Roku	http://www.roku.com
Smith Micro Vidio	http://www.smithmicro.com/products/vidio.aspx
Sonic Foundry	http://www.sonicfoundry.com
TANDBERG	http://www.tandberg.com
TelecomTV	http://www.telecomtv.com
TubeMogul	http://www.tubemogul.com
Ustream	http://www.ustream.tv
VBrick	http://www.vbrick.com

Viddler	http://www.viddler.com
VideoPress	http://www.videopress.com
VideoSurf	http://www.videosurf.com
Vidyo	http://www.vidyo.com
Vimeo	http://www.vimeo.com
VYou	http://www.vyou.com
WebM	http://www.webmproject.org
Windows Live Movie Maker	http://explore.live.com/windows-live-movie-maker?os=other
YouTube	http://www.youtube.com
YuMe	http://www.yume.com

VIRTUALIZATION

AppSense	http://www.appsense.com
Astute Networks	http://www.astutenetworks.com
Azul Systems	http://www.azulsystems.com
Citrix Xen Solutions	http://www.xensource.com
Microsoft Virtual PC	http://www.microsoft.com/windows/virtual-pc/
Microsoft Virtualization	http://www.microsoft.com/virtualization/

Parallels	http://www.parallels.com
Reflex Systems	http://www.reflexsystems.com
RES Software	http://www.ressoftware.com
Sanbolic	http://www.sanbolic.com
ScaleMP	http://www.scalemp.com
Veeam	http://www.veeam.com
VirtualBox	http://www.virtualbox.org
VM6 Software	http://www.vm6software.com
VMware	http://www.vmware.com
Xen	http://www.xen.org
Xsigo	http://www.xsigo.com

WEB BROWSER

Amaya	http://www.w3.org/Amaya/
Apple Safari	http://www.apple.com/safari/
Bolt Browser	http://www.boltbrowser.com
Buddy Browser	http://www.buddybrowser.com
Camino	http://www.caminobrowser.org

Google Chrome	http://www.google.com/chrome/
Kinoma	http://www.kinoma.com
Maxthon	http://www.maxthon.com
Microsoft Internet Explorer	http://www.microsoft.com/ie/
Midori Web Browser	http://www.twotoasts.de
Mozilla Firefox	http://www.mozilla.com
NetSurf	http://www.netsurf-browser.org
Opera	http://www.opera.com
Personas	http://www.getpersonas.com
SeaMonkey	http://www.seamonkey-project.org
Skyfire	http://www.skyfire.com
Viigo	http://www.viigo.com

WEB TECHNOLOGY

3Scale	http://www.3scale.net
Adobe AIR	http://www.adobe.com/products/air/
Adobe ColdFusion	http://www.adobe.com/products/coldfusion/
Adobe Flex	http://www.adobe.com/products/flex/

Ajaxian	http://www.ajaxian.com
Akamai	http://www.akamai.com
Alexa	http://www.alexa.com
Apache Axis2	http://axis.apache.org/axis2/java/core/
Apache Tomcat	http://tomcat.apache.org/
APE Ajax Push Engine	http://www.ape-project.org
ASP.NET	http://www.asp.net
ASP.NET MVC	http://www.asp.net/mvc
Beautyoftheweb.com	http://www.beautyoftheweb.com
BitNami	http://www.bitnami.org
BlogEngine.NET	http://www.dotnetblogengine.net
Blogger	http://www.blogger.com
BookingBug	http://www.bookingbug.com
BuyDomains.com	http://www.buydomains.com
Calais	http://www.opencalais.com
ChronoForms	http://www.chronoengine.com
Cint	http://www.cint.com
CiviCRM	http://www.civicrm.org

cPanel	http://www.cpanel.net
DHTML	http://www.w3schools.com/dhtml/default.asp
DISQUS	http://www.disqus.com
Django	http://www.djangoproject.com
Docstoc	http://www.docstoc.com
Dojo Toolkit	http://www.dojotoolkit.org
Ektron	http://www.ektron.com
Elance	http://www.elance.com
Embedly	http://www.embed.ly
ExpressionEngine	http://www.expressionengine.com
Fetch Technologies	http://www.fetch.com
Firebug	http://www.getfirebug.com
Go Daddy	http://www.godaddy.com
GoodData	http://www.gooddata.com
Google +1 Button	http://www.google.com/+1/button/
Google Analytics	http://www.google.com/analytics/
Google Sites	http://sites.google.com/
Google Web Toolkit	http://code.google.com/webtoolkit/

Grails	http://www.grails.org
Grok	http://grok.zope.org/
HTML	http://w3schools.com/html/
IBM WebSphere	http://www.ibm.com/software/websphere/
ICEFaces	http://www.icefaces.org
InVision	http://www.invisionapp.com
ipadio	http://www.ipadio.com
Jide	http://www.jide.fr
jQuery	http://www.jquery.com
JSON – Javascript Object Notation	http://www.json.org
JumpTime	http://www.jumptime.com
Kontagent	http://www.kontagent.com
Liferay	http://www.liferay.com
LiveChat	http://www.livechatinc.com
Mahara	http://www.mahara.org
Managing News	http://www.managingnews.com
Mashape	http://www.mashape.com
Mashery	http://www.mashery.com

Microsoft IIS - Internet Information Services	http://www.iis.net
Microsoft WebMatrix	http://www.microsoft.com/web/webmatrix/
Mixpanel Analytics	http://www.mixpanel.com
ModSecurity	http://www.modsecurity.org
MojoMotor	http://www.mojomotor.com
mojoPortal	http://www.mojoportal.com
MooTools	http://www.mootools.net
myGengo	http://www.mygengo.com
Name.com	http://www.name.com
NetDNA	http://www.netdna.com
NetworkedBlogs	http://www.networkedblogs.com
New Relic	http://www.newrelic.com
Open Atrium	http://www.openatrium.com
OpenId	http://www.openid.net
OpenPublish	http://www.openpublishapp.com
Orchard	http://www.orchardproject.net
Parallels Plesk Panel	http://www.parallels.com/plesk/

Posterous	https://www.posterous.com
Quantcast	http://www.quantcast.com
reCAPTCHA	http://www.google.com/recaptcha
RoboForm	http://www.roboform.com
RSS Graffiti	http://www.rssgraffiti.com
RSSBus	http://www.rssbus.com
Schema.org	http://www.schema.org
ScrewTurn Wiki	http://www.screwturn.eu
ScribeSEO	http://www.scribeseo.com
script.aculo.us	http://script.aculo.us/
Sencha	http://www.sencha.com
simplejson	http://pypi.python.org/pypi/simplejson/
Site Meter	http://www.sitemeter.com
Site24x7	http://www.site24x7.com
Sitelock	http://www.sitelock.com
Spring Roo	http://www.springsource.org/roo
Spring Web Flow	http://www.springsource.org/webflow
Squarespace	http://www.squarespace.com

Squid	http://www.squid-cache.org
SurveyGizmo	http://www.surveygizmo.com
SurveyMonkey	http://www.surveymonkey.com
Tornado	http://www.tornadoweb.org
TypePad	http://www.typepad.com
Varnish Cache	http://www.varnish-cache.org
vBulletin	http://www.vbulletin.com
Visual WebGui	http://www.visualwebgui.com
WebPlus	http://www.serif.com/webplus/
Webtrends	http://www.webtrends.com
Wix.com	http://www.wix.com
WordPress	http://www.wordpress.org
Wufoo	http://www.wufoo.com
XHTML	http://www.w3schools.com/xhtml/
Yahoo! WebPlayer	http://webplayer.yahoo.com/
YUI	http://developer.yahoo.com/yui/
ZK	http://www.zkoss.org
Zoho	http://www.zoho.com

Zope	http://www.zope.org

WIRELESS

Alvarion	http://www.alvarion.com
AnaCom	http://www.anacominc.com
Antamedia	http://www.antamedia.com
Aruba Networks	http://www.arubanetworks.com
Axxcelera	http://www.axxcelera.com
Belkin	http://www.belkin.com
BridgeWave	http://www.bridgewave.com
Ceragon	http://www.ceragon.com
CML Microcircuit	http://www.cmlmicro.com
Hughes Network Systems	http://www.hughes.com
LM Technologies	http://www.lm-technologies.com
Meru Networks	http://www.merunetworks.com
Novatel Wireless	http://www.novatelwireless.com
Powerwave	http://www.powerwave.com
Proxim Wireless	http://www.proxim.com

Q-KON	http://www.qkon.com
RADIO FREQUENCY SYSTEMS (RFS)	http://www.rfsworld.com
Radio Waves	http://www.radiowavesinc.com
RADWIN	http://www.radwin.com
RF Micro Devices	http://www.rfmd.com
Satel	http://www.satel.com
SkyPilot	http://skypilot.trilliantinc.com/
Tropos	http://www.tropos.com
WAVION	http://www.wavionnetworks.com
Winncom	http://www.winncom.com
Xirrus	http://www.xirrus.com

XML

Altova	http://www.altova.com
Extensible Markup Language (XML)	http://www.w3.org/XML/
IBM developerWorks XML	http://www.ibm.com/developerworks/xml/
PHP XML WRITER	http://www.php.net/xmlwriter

Stylus Studio	http://www.stylusstudio.com
Xiph.org	http://www.xiph.org
XML Pro	http://www.vervet.com
XML Query	http://www.w3schools.com/xquery/default.asp
XML.com	http://www.xml.com
XML.org	http://www.xml.org
XMPP Standards Foundation	http://www.xmpp.org
Xquery	http://www.w3.org/TR/xquery/

www.ingramcontent.com/pod-product-compliance
Lightning Source LLC
Chambersburg PA
CBHW071201050326
40689CB00011B/2202